# HEALTHY SNACKS FOR KIDS
## REVISED EDITION

**Penny Warner**

BRISTOL PUBLISHING ENTERPRISES
San Leandro, California

# a nitty gritty® cookbook

Printed in the United States of America.

ISBN 1-55867-159-5

Cover design: Frank J. Paredes
Cover photography: John A. Benson
Food stylist: Merilee Hague Bordin
Illustrator: James Balkovek

# CONTENTS

# SMUGGLE GOOD THINGS
# INTO EVERY MEAL

"Snack time!" The words are magic to a child's ear. But to a parent, they can present a real challenge. You may reach a point when you don't know what to do to get your child to eat nutritious foods. Try as you might to introduce high fiber foods and leafy greens, your child refuses to have any part of them. Maybe those prepackaged cookies and chips aren't so bad. After all, a child has to eat something!

There is plenty of evidence that nutrition is important for good health now and later in life. Studies even indicate that eating the right foods prevents some diseases. You will give your child the gift of better health if you encourage healthy eating habits that he or she can carry into the future.

When all else fails, try trickery! Be sneaky with the picky eater and pump up breakfasts, snacks and meals with nutritious ingredients. Your child will develop a taste for healthy foods and you will gradually influence and encourage healthy eating.

With the help of the many ideas and recipes in this collection, you can establish a lifetime of good eating habits for your child. To make your job easier, the recipes in this book are high in nutrition, easy to prepare, inexpensive, low in or free of sugar and salt and loved by kids.

# TEN WAYS TO MAKE YOUR CHILD A HEALTHY EATER

## 1. Smuggle nutritious foods into old favorites.

Mix chopped spinach into turkey burgers, grated carrots into peanut butter and cooked zucchini into pancakes. Add a little wheat germ to pizza dough, cookies and even smoothies. Be creative with your trickery — you'll surprise yourself.

## 2. Give food silly names.

Children love whimsical things and will usually try something new if it has a funny name. What kid could resist a glass of "Mooseberry Juice" or a "Banana Wiggle"?

## 3. Let kids help.

Even small children can help in the preparation of some of the things they eat. Children who help make their snacks are more likely to eat them. Better yet, teach children how to grow their own vegetables in the backyard garden.

## 4. Educate your child about the food pyramid.

Talk about foods that help children grow strong and stay healthy — and those that don't. Classify foods at the market or on the table into the five food groups of the food pyramid. Play simple games that teach about these foods.

## 5. Think small.

It's not so overwhelming to a child when there are small amounts on a plate, or small bites to eat. A child will ask for more if desired. Sometimes it's fun to make a face or a design with the food. Try anything to create a happy atmosphere and stimulate a child's imagination.

## 6. Go easy on sugar and salt.

Try to omit sugar and salt from the recipes you make, or at least decrease the amount used. The results may not taste as good to you, but if your child is raised with limited amounts of sugar and salt, she or he will never miss them. Use alternatives, such as dates and raisins, whenever possible. If you feel you must use a sweetener, use honey instead of sugar — it's sweeter so you don't need to use as much. Keep salt and sugar off the table, and look for unsweetened products at the market.

## 7. Let props help sell what you're serving.

Kids love bright colors, animals, clowns, funny straws and above all, variety. A different plate or a funny bowl with a picture on it just might stimulate a child's desire to try something new. Avoid the same old thing. Collect a variety of small colorful plates, cups, bowls, glasses and place mats.

## 8.  Make mealtime and snack time a pleasant social event.

A child is much more apt to try new things under these circumstances. Don't get angry — it only makes a child more stubborn. Maybe he or she simply isn't hungry, but will be a willing eater at the next meal. Try to avoid pleading ("Please eat"), threatening ("No dessert if you don't eat your salad") or guilt-inducing ("Think of all the hungry children in the world"). These tactics won't help in the long run. Ask your child to try everything. Don't force him or her to finish everything.

## 9.  Don't neglect dairy products.

Substitute low fat or nonfat dairy products for those made with whole milk. Use reduced fat or nonfat cheeses, especially when there are several other ingredients in a recipe. Experiment with nonfat cheeses to find those that melt well. Some regular cheeses are naturally lower in fat, such as part-skim mozzarella and Parmesan.

## 10. Cut back on fats.

Turkey lunch meats are good low fat substitutes for bologna, salami and other lunch meats. When a recipe calls for nuts or seeds, you may want to reduce the quantity (they have lots of fiber, but unfortunately are high in fat). You'll find that cutting back on the fats in a recipe frequently doesn't affect the overall flavor!

# FOOD PYRAMID

**Fats, Oils and Sweets**
Use sparingly

**Milk, Cheese and Yogurt Group**
2 to 3 servings

**Meat, Poultry, Fish, Dry Beans, Eggs and Nuts Group**
2 to 3 servings

**Vegetable Group**
3 to 5 servings

**Fruit Group**
2 to 4 servings

**Bread, Cereal, Rice and Pasta Group**
6 to 11 servings

# SERVING SIZES

**Milk group**: 1 cup milk or yogurt, 1½ oz. natural cheese, or 2 oz. processed cheese.

**Meat group**: 2 to 3 oz. cooked lean meat, poultry or fish — about the size of a deck of cards. The following choices count as 1 oz. meat: ½ cup cooked dry beans, 1 egg, 2 tbs. peanut butter or ⅓ cup nuts. Do not serve nuts to children under the age of two, because they are a choking hazard.

**Vegetable group**: 1 cup raw leafy vegetables, ½ cup chopped cooked or raw vegetables, ¾ cup vegetable juice.

**Fruit group**: 1 medium piece of fruit, ½ cup mixed fruit or ¾ cup fruit juice.

**Bread group:** 1 slice bread, ½ bagel or English muffin, 1 oz. cold cereal, ½ cup cooked cereal, ½ cup rice or pasta or 5 to 6 small crackers.

# THE BASICS OF HEALTHY EATING

This is a list of good basic foods children should be encouraged to eat. If a child learns to enjoy them early, he or she will be a healthy eater for life.

Use these foods interchangeably in the recipes in this book, and use the recipes as a guideline for your own ideas. For example, instead of sneaking spinach into turkey burgers (*Popeye Burgers*, page 158), hide pureed peas or green beans in meat loaf mix.

## Bread, Cereal, Rice and Pasta Group

- air-popped popcorn
- bagels
- bran cereals
- brown rice
- cornbread
- crackers
- English muffins
- low fat granola
- macaroni
- oatmeal
- spaghetti
- whole grain breads

## Vegetable Group

- broccoli
- carrots
- cauliflower
- celery
- corn
- fresh beans
- green bell peppers
- peas
- potatoes
- red bell peppers
- spinach
- squash
- sweet potatoes
- tomatoes
- zucchini

## Fruit Group

- apricots
- berries
- cherries
- citrus fruits
- dried fruits
- kiwis
- mangoes
- melons
- papayas
- peaches
- pears
- pineapples
- plums
- prunes

## Milk, Cheese and Yogurt Group

- buttermilk
- low fat cottage cheese
- low fat fruit-flavored yogurt
- ice milk
- low fat or nonfat milk
- low fat ricotta cheese
- Parmesan cheese
- part-skim mozzarella cheese
- yogurt cheese

## Meat, Poultry, Fish, Dry Beans, Eggs and Nuts Group

- chicken
- extra-lean ham
- peanuts or reduced fat peanut butter
- lean beef
- lentils
- split peas
- beans: pinto, kidney, garbanzo, etc.
- shrimp
- tofu
- water-packed tuna
- turkey
- walnuts

# HEALTHFUL HINTS

- Children must eat often due to their bodies' demand for high energy. Serve them 3 meals and 2 to 3 healthy snacks each day on a regular schedule. Don't overdo it, however. Children should learn to experience hunger instead of constantly feeling full.

- Carob is a good substitute for chocolate because it doesn't contain caffeine.

- Whole wheat flour can be substituted for white flour in most recipes. If you don't want to use all whole wheat, replace part of the white flour with whole wheat flour. You will be adding important fiber to your family's diet. Use whole grain bread whenever possible.

- Use yogurt cheese instead of cream cheese: Drain 1 qt. nonfat, gelatin-free plain yogurt in a yogurt cheese maker or through a paper coffee filter suspended in a tall container. Refrigerate for 24 hours or until thick. Discard the liquid (whey). Makes about 2 cups.

- Emphasize citrus fruits in your child's diet. They are rich in vitamin C and provide important nutrients for growing bodies. Try one of the calcium-fortified orange juices on the market for strengthening little bones. Whenever possible, opt for whole fruits instead of fruit juices to add fiber.

- Look for fruits and vegetables that are brilliantly colored. A good rule of thumb is that the brighter in color the fruit or vegetable, the more nutrients it contains. For example, choose romaine lettuce instead of iceberg because its green color is much deeper.

- Use only one high fat ingredient in each dish. Nonfat items are good choices for mixing with several other ingredients in a recipe. The other flavors in the dish compensate for blandness.

- Use refrigerated pizza dough instead of biscuit dough when making pigs-in-a-blanket or other children's favorites. Biscuit dough gets about 50% of its calories from fat, while pizza dough derives only 14% of its calories from fat.

- Dairy products are important for a young person's growth. If you select milk products that are low fat or nonfat, your child will get all of the benefits of dairy without unneeded fat and cholesterol. Hard cheeses are generally more flavorful, so you don't need to use as much.

- The most important thing you can do to make your child a healthy eater is to set a good example. Kids watch their parents for clues on how to behave. If you don't eat well, it's unreasonable to expect them to do so.

# HAVE FUN WITH FEEDING

- Make toast faces: spread toast with yogurt cheese or peanut butter, and use nuts, raisins, coconut, dried fruit bits or pieces of vegetables to make faces.
- If your child carries a lunch box, tuck in a surprise: a new pencil, a cheerful note, a fancy straw — use your imagination.
- Use cookie cutters to cut out bread for fanciful sandwiches.
- Splurge on some bright paper products; colorful cartons, straws and napkins dress up a meal or a snack.
- Add pleasant music to mealtime or snack time. Discourage television viewing while children are eating.
- Stuff sandwich fillings into different edible holders. Bell peppers, cored apples, ice cream cones, waffle squares, cooked giant pasta shells, pancakes, hollowed tomatoes and hollowed dinner rolls are all fun choices.
- Make cottage cheese or yogurt "sundaes" in cantaloupe or honeydew melon halves. Top with granola and a cherry.
- Make "boats" out of raw snow pea pods and fill with sandwich fillings. Make "sails" out of green bell pepper pieces.

## NUTRITIONAL ANALYSIS

This book offers a brief nutritional analysis for each recipe*. The analysis is presented for the smallest number of servings indicated in each recipe unless otherwise specified. Optional ingredients are not calculated in the analysis. If a choice of ingredients is offered, the first ingredient is analyzed. For recipes using yogurt cheese, refer to the recipe on page 9.

A graphic representation of the food pyramid is shown for each recipe, indicating the food group(s) that is emphasized. This does not mean that that group's servings are adequate for the day, but only that the group is represented in this recipe.

*Recipes were analyzed using **The Food Processor II**, available from ESHA Research, P.O. Box 13028, Salem, OR 97309.

## FAT INTAKE

Opinions differ on the amount of fat calories youngsters should eat. Some authorities recommend that they keep their fat intake between 30% and 40% of their daily calories. Other experts, however, recommend that children, like adults, should consume no more than 30% of their daily calories in the form of fat. Most agree that parents should not restrict fat intake for children under 2 years.

# SUPER SNACKS

# MAKE DELICIOUS SNACKS QUICKLY AND EASILY

Snacks are an important and necessary part of a child's life. Because of the enormous amounts of energy used, little bodies need refueling between meals. This important role that snacks play in keeping children healthy makes it all the more necessary that snacks be as nutritious as possible, and something your child will love to eat.

Since foods that are good for children are not necessarily the ones they will eat, the carefully chosen snacks in this chapter pack a lot of extra nutrition into good foods kids do like, and hide less popular ones in old favorites.

These delicious snacks are great anytime: mid-morning, after school, before a late dinner and at bedtime. They are also great additions to breakfast, lunch and dinner.

With the wide variety of recipes in this chapter, you'll have enough new snacks to last a long time!

# FRUIT BRICKS

*Children can play with this snack and eat it too! For variety, use apple or grape juice concentrate. Gelatin is pure protein that has been derived from animals.*

3 pkg. (1/4 oz. each) unflavored gelatin
3/4 cup boiling water
1 can (12 oz.) frozen orange juice
    concentrate

    Dissolve gelatin in boiling water. Add concentrate and stir until mixed. Lightly spray a 9-x-13-inch pan with nonstick cooking spray. Pour mixture into pan. Chill for several hours. Cut into squares for building blocks or use cookie cutters to make interesting shapes.

***per recipe***    *61 calories, 26.1 g protein, 130 g carbo., 0.7 g fat, 1% calories from fat*

# MUNCHKINS

*Tease little taste buds with bundles of fruit and nuts.*

1½ cups boiling water
1 cup chopped dried apricots
¼ cup raisins
½ cup chopped pecans
2 tbs. orange juice

In a bowl, pour boiling water over apricots and raisins and set aside for 30 minutes. Drain well. Mix in pecans and orange juice. Shape into balls and refrigerate. Makes 12 balls.

***per ball*** *66 calories, 0.9 g protein, 10.1 g carbo., 3.1 g fat, 39% calories from fat*

# SIDEWALK MIX

*There aren't a lot of trails in the suburbs, so we call it "sidewalk mix." Peanuts provide protein and coconut provides potassium, but both are high in fat. Reduce the amounts if desired.*

2 cups low fat granola
½ cup unsweetened shredded coconut
½ cup chopped dates
¼ cup chopped peanuts
2 tbs. honey, if desired

Mix all ingredients and press into an 8-inch square pan. Break into small pieces. Or, omit honey and serve in a large bowl. Makes 4 servings.

*per serving*   *428 calories, 9 g protein, 58 g carbo., 21 g fat, 41% calories from fat*

# HOT NIBBLES

*Dried fruit and oats provide lots of carbohydrates and fiber. Fat can be minimized by reducing or omitting the sunflower kernels and the coconut.*

1 tbs. reduced fat margarine, melted
¼ cup chopped dried apricots
¼ cup raisins
¼ cup sunflower kernels
¼ cup unsweetened shredded coconut
¼ cup chopped dates
¼ cup rolled oats

Stir ingredients together in a skillet until heated through. Serve warm. Makes 6 servings.

*per serving*   *133 calories, 2.7 g protein, 17.7 g carbo., 6.8 g fat, 43% calories from fat*

# CUPCONES

*These go over big at birthday or classroom parties. Garnish them with coconut, raisins or crushed cereal. Reduce fat by using reduced fat peanut butter and nonfat (skim) milk.*

24 ice cream cup cones
½ cup peanut butter
⅓ cup margarine
2-4 tbs. honey
2 eggs
1 tsp. vanilla extract

2 cups flour
½ tsp. salt
2½ tsp. baking powder
¾ cup 2% milk
jam or yogurt

Place cones in muffin cups. Combine peanut butter and margarine. Add honey and beat until fluffy. Beat in eggs and vanilla extract. Add flour, salt, baking powder and milk. Beat until mixed. Spoon into cones to about ¼-inch from the top. Bake at 350° for 25 minutes. Frost with jam or yogurt. Makes 24 servings.

*per serving*   *128 calories, 3.5 g protein, 12 g carbo., 6 g fat, 42% calories from fat*

# PEANUT BUTTER POPCORN

*This old favorite has lots of fiber. Serve with plenty of napkins.*

1 tbs. peanut butter
1 tbs. reduced fat margarine
2 qt. air-popped popcorn

Melt peanut butter and margarine in a small pan over low heat. Pour over popcorn. Toss to mix well. Makes 8 servings.

---

***per cup***   *52 calories, 1.5 g protein, 6.5 g carbo., 1.8 g fat, 31% calories from fat*

# FRUITY POPCORN

*Plop them down with their favorite movie and this extra-special popcorn when it's too rainy to play outside.*

¼ cup honey
¼ cup water
¼ cup reduced fat margarine
1 tbs. vanilla extract
½ tsp. salt

1 tsp. wheat germ
1 qt. air-popped popcorn
1 cup raisins
1 cup chopped dried apricots
1 cup sunflower kernels

Stir honey and water together over medium heat until a candy thermometer registers 250°. Add margarine, vanilla extract, salt and wheat germ. Pour over popcorn in a large bowl and mix well. Spread mixture into a large baking pan. Bake at 300° for 15 minutes. Remove from oven. Combine raisins, apricots and sunflower kernels. Stir in popcorn mixture. Place mixture in pan and bake 15 minutes longer. Cool and serve in small bowls or sacks, or form into small balls. Makes 8 servings.

*per cup*   *282 calories, 5.9 g protein, 39.5 g carbo., 13.6 g fat, 40% calories from fat*

# DATE COOKIES

*If you feel that jam and jelly are too high in sugar, try a pure fruit spread. Reduce the fat calories by cutting back on walnuts.*

1 cup chopped dates
1 cup graham cracker crumbs
¼ cup plum or strawberry jam
½ cup chopped walnuts
½ cup unsweetened shredded coconut

Combine dates, crumbs, jam and nuts. Drop by teaspoonfuls into a bowl of coconut and roll into balls. Cover and chill. Makes 24 cookies.

*per cookie*    *63 calories, 0.7 g protein, 9.9 g carbo., 2.8 g fat, 37% calories from fat*

# PEANUT BUTTER MUFFINS

*If they refuse to eat sandwiches, try this sneak attack. Cut the fat calories further with nonfat (skim) milk and reduced fat peanut butter.*

1/3 cup brown sugar, firmly packed
1/3 cup peanut butter
1 egg
1/4 cup shredded carrots
3/4 cup flour

1/4 cup rolled oats
1 tsp. baking powder
1/4 tsp. baking soda
1/8 tsp. salt
1/2 cup 2% milk

Beat brown sugar and peanut butter; add egg and beat well. Stir in carrots. Add flour, oats, baking powder, soda, salt and milk, and beat until just blended. Pour into paper-lined muffin cups and bake at 400° for 15 to 20 minutes or until golden. Makes 8 to 10 muffins.

---

***per muffin*** *168 calories, 5.6 g protein, 22.9 g carbo., 6.5 g fat, 34% calories from fat*

# JACK'S BEANSTALKS

*Cheese and beans make a high-protein snack for after-school nibblers.*

1 can (16 oz.) kidney beans
1/2 cup grated cheddar cheese
1/2 tsp. chili powder, if desired
8 celery stalks

Drain beans and save a little liquid. Mash beans with a fork, or process with a food processor or blender, adding a little bean liquid for a creamier texture. Stir in cheese and chili powder, if using. Simmer mixture in a small saucepan over low heat until cheese melts. Refrigerate. When cooled, stuff celery stalks with mixture. Cut into bite-sized pieces. Keep refrigerated in airtight containers. Makes 8 servings.

***per serving*** *83 calories, 5 g protein, 10.5 g carbo., 2.6 g fat, 27% calories from fat*

# SPUMONI CELERY

*Here's a tricky way to cover the vegetable group. Try other combinations for variety.*

1 carrot, finely chopped
1/4 cup finely chopped green bell pepper
1/2 cup low fat cottage cheese
1/4 cup grated Parmesan cheese
6 celery stalks, cut into 3- to 4-inch pieces

Mix carrot, green pepper, cottage cheese and Parmesan together well. Stuff celery pieces. Makes 6 servings.

*per serving*   *49 calories, 4.8 g protein, 3.8 g carbo., 1.7 g fat, 31% calories from fat*

# BANANA WIGGLES

*Gelatin is such a good package for presenting food to kids, and it's high in protein too. You can make inexpensive popsicles out of juice cans, popsicle sticks and aluminum foil.*

1½ pkg. (¼ oz. each) unflavored gelatin
1 cup boiling water
¾ cup cold water

1 cup strawberry puree or
    strawberry nectar
3 bananas

Dissolve gelatin in boiling water. Add cold water and strawberry puree. Chill in refrigerator until slightly thickened. Cut bananas in half crosswise. Insert a popsicle stick in the flat end of each banana. Place bananas in empty juice cans or large plastic cups, sticks up. Pour in gelatin mixture. To keep sticks centered, place foil over the top of each can with a small slit in the center of each cover for sticks. Chill in refrigerator for several hours. To loosen, dip cans in warm water for a few seconds. Wiggle gently to remove. Makes 6 servings.

*per serving*   *67 calories, 2.2 g protein, 15.6 g carbo., 0.3 g fat, 4% calories from fat*

# BANANA OATSIES

*These fruit and cereal snacks are great to make when you're short on time. Cut the amount of walnuts to further reduce fat.*

4 bananas
½ cup rolled oats
¾ cup chopped walnuts
¾ cup Grape Nuts cereal
1 tsp. vanilla extract

Mash bananas and add remaining ingredients. Mix well. Drop by teaspoonfuls onto an ungreased cookie sheet. Bake at 350° for 20 to 25 minutes. Makes 30 cookies.

---

***per cookie***   *49 calories, 1.1 g protein, 7.4 g carbo., 2 g fat, 35% calories from fat*

# FRUIT COBBLER CRUNCH

*This is a quick and easy way to serve fruit. Use fruits canned in their own juice without added sugar.*

1 can (8 oz.) peaches, pears, apricots or plums in juice
1 tsp. cinnamon
2 tbs. low fat granola
2 tbs. plain (or fruit) low fat yogurt

Drain fruit. Slice into 2 serving dishes. Sprinkle with cinnamon. Add granola and top with yogurt. Makes 2 servings.

***per serving*** *101 calories, 1.9 g protein, 21.8 g carbo., 1.4 g fat, 12% calories from fat*

# PITA PARFAIT

*How about a "fruit sandwich"?*

1 can (8 oz.) fruit cocktail, drained
2 tbs. low fat cottage cheese
1 tbs. chopped almonds or walnuts
1 pita bread

Mix fruit with cottage cheese and nuts. Cut pita bread in half to make 2 pockets. Spoon fruit mixture into pita pockets. Makes 2 servings.

*per serving*   *172 calories, 6.1 g protein, 31.2 g carbo., 3 g fat, 16% calories from fat*

# OVEN APPLES

*These child-sized baked apples are perfect at breakfast, lunch, dinner or snack time.*

4 small baking apples
2 tbs. chopped walnuts
2 tbs. raisins
1 tsp. cinnamon

Cut apples in half and hollow core. Place in a baking pan. Combine nuts, raisins and cinnamon in a small bowl. Stuff mixture into apple hollows. Cover and bake at 350° for 30 minutes. Serve warm, at room temperature or chilled. Makes 8 servings.

*per serving*   *62 calories, 0.5 g protein, 13.2 g carbo., 1.4 g fat, 19% calories from fat*

# SUPER-HERO SNACKS

*These provide lots of energy for ambitious youngsters. Reduce fat by using egg substitute instead of eggs. Eggs get about 60% of their calories from fat, while egg substitute, made mostly of egg whites, gets about 37% of its calories from fat. Use ¼ cup egg substitute for each large egg.*

2 eggs
½ cup unsweetened applesauce
2 cups low fat granola

Beat eggs well and blend into applesauce. Add granola and mix well. Spray an 8-inch square pan lightly with nonstick cooking spray. Press mixture firmly and evenly into pan. Bake at 350° for 20 minutes. Cut into bars and serve. Makes 9 bars.

*per bar*   *134 calories, 4 g protein, 18.4 g carbo., 5.5 g fat, 37% calories from fat*

# APPLE SMACKS

*Served warm or cold, these are always a favorite. Top them with yogurt if desired.*

4 apples, sliced
¼ cup raisins
¼ cup water
¾ cup rolled oats
⅓ cup flour

¼ cup wheat germ
¼ cup margarine
2 tbs. honey, if desired
1 tsp. cinnamon

Spray an 8-inch square pan with nonstick cooking spray. Lay apple slices in pan. Combine remaining ingredients and sprinkle over apples. Bake at 350° for 35 minutes. Spoon into small dishes. Makes 4 servings.

*per serving*   *365 calories, 5.7 g protein, 59.3 g carbo., 13.6 g fat, 32% calories from fat*

# YOGURT PLUS

*Here's an easy way to cover the food pyramid in one delicious snack! The following are suggestions. Experiment with your own ideas. Use nuts and seeds sparingly, as they have naturally occurring fat.*

**Start with 8 oz. plain (or vanilla) low fat yogurt. Add one of the following from each group.**

## Fruits

- sliced strawberries
- raspberries
- blueberries
- chopped apricots, fresh or dried
- chopped apples
- sliced bananas
- sectioned oranges

- raisins or other dried fruits
- chopped dates
- halved grapes
- sliced kiwi
- cubed melon
- sliced peaches
- diced pineapple

## Vegetables

- shredded carrots
- diced celery
- chopped cucumber
- chopped red or yellow bell pepper
- diced tomato
- sliced jicama

## Nuts and Seeds

- sunflower kernels
- sliced almonds
- sesame seeds
- reduced fat peanut butter
- chopped walnuts

## Grains and Cereals

- cooked brown rice
- puffed rice
- Grape Nuts cereal
- low fat granola
- whole wheat toast pieces
- wheat germ
- bran flakes
- crushed shredded wheat cereal

# HOT CHEESE FUNNIES

*This is a New York City special! Let the kids experiment by making up their own shapes. Decrease fat calories with reduced-fat or nonfat cheddar.*

1 pkg. active dry yeast
1½ cups warm water (105° to 115°)
3½ cups flour
1 cup grated cheddar cheese
1 egg, beaten

Dissolve yeast in water. Stir in flour and cheese. Knead dough until smooth. (If the dough is too sticky, add more flour a teaspoon at a time.) Break off walnut-sized pieces and roll into 12-inch long ropes. Twist into pretzel shapes. Place shapes on an ungreased cookie sheet and brush with egg. Bake at 425° for 15 to 20 minutes. Serve warm. Makes about 30.

*per pretzel*   *41 calories, 1.9 g protein, 4.9 g carbo., 1.5 g fat, 33% calories from fat*

# FRUIT CHEWIES

*These snacks are high in fiber and naturally sweet. Reduce the amount of nuts, if desired, to lower the recipe's fat.*

3 bananas
1 cup chopped dates
¼ cup canola oil
2 cups rolled oats
½ cup chopped walnuts, peanuts or pecans
1 tsp. vanilla extract

Cut 2 of the bananas into medium-sized chunks. Mash 1 banana. Combine all ingredients and stir until mixed. Let stand for 10 minutes. Drop by teaspoonfuls onto a greased cookie sheet. Bake at 350° for 15 to 20 minutes. Makes 24 cookies.

*per cookie*   95 calories, 1.7 g protein, 13.8 g carbo., 4.3 g fat, 39% calories from fat

# APRICOTTIES

*These cookies are high in vitamin A, vitamin C and fiber. Fat can be reduced by using egg substitute and/or cutting back on sunflower kernels.*

½ cup chopped dried apricots
½ cup raisins
½ cup chopped dates
1 can (6 oz.) frozen orange juice
    concentrate
1½ cups rolled oats

1 cup flour
1 tsp. baking soda
dash salt
1 egg
½ cup canola oil
¼ cup sunflower kernels

Combine fruit and concentrate in a saucepan. Simmer for 10 minutes, stirring occasionally. Cool. Stir together oats, flour, baking soda, salt, egg and oil. Stir in fruit mixture and kernels. Form into small balls and place on a foil-lined baking sheet. Flatten balls into ¼-inch disks and bake at 350° for 10 minutes. Makes 18 cookies.

---

***per cookie***    *103 calories, 1.9 g protein, 14 g carbo., 4.7 g fat, 40% calories from fat*

# HAWAIIAN ROLLERS

*Feed this energy-giving snack to a hungry soccer team. Since it's so quick and easy, why not double the recipe?*

1 can (10 oz.) refrigerated pizza dough
½ cup pineapple preserves
½ tsp. cinnamon
¼ cup unsweetened coconut
¼ cup chopped walnuts

Cut dough into 2 rectangles. Divide preserves and spread evenly over each rectangle. Sprinkle evenly with cinnamon, coconut and nuts. Roll up dough jelly roll-style and seal the edges. Cut each roll into 12 slices. Place slices cut-side up on an ungreased cookie sheet. Bake at 400° for 10 minutes. Serve warm or cooled. Makes 24 slices.

*per slice*   *45 calories, 1.3 g protein, 6.4 g carbo., 1.7 g fat, 35% calories from fat*

# BANANA BOMBS

*These are great for outings and picnics.*

1 cup flour
½ tsp. baking soda
½ tsp. salt, if desired
½ cup chopped nuts or seeds

1 banana, cut into small chunks
½ cup chopped dates
1 egg
1 tsp. vanilla extract

Combine flour, soda, salt, if using, and nuts in a bowl. Combine banana, dates, egg and vanilla extract in a blender container. Blend until smooth. Add to dry ingredients and mix well. Drop by teaspoonfuls onto a greased cookie sheet. Flatten with the back of a spoon. Bake at 350° for 10 minutes. Makes 24 cookies.

*per cookie*   *43 calories, 1.3 g protein, 5.8 g carbo., 1.8 g fat, 35% calories from fat*

# FLYING SAUCERS

*Feed these to your little space-walkers.*

1 pkg. (10 oz.) refrigerated pizza dough
1 cup cooked ground turkey
½ cup grated Swiss cheese
½ cup frozen tiny peas, thawed
2 tbs. reduced fat mayonnaise
1 tbs. mustard

Cut dough into 8 equal pieces. Shape each piece into a ball, and flatten each ball to form a 4-inch disk. Combine remaining ingredients and divide among half of the disks. Top with remaining disks and seal edges closed with the tines of a fork. Bake at 375° for 15 to 20 minutes or until golden brown. Serve warm. Makes 4 servings.

*per serving*   325 calories, 18 g protein, 36.6 g carbo., 11.5 g fat, 32% calories from fat

# MONKEY BARS

*These cookie bars provide sustenance for playground antics.*

½ cup reduced fat margarine
¼ cup honey, or less if desired
1 egg
¼ tsp. cinnamon
1 banana, sliced
4 cups rolled oats

½ cup chopped dried apricots
½ cup chopped prunes
½ cup raisins
½ cup chopped walnuts
½ cup sunflower kernels

Beat margarine and honey until light and fluffy. Add egg, cinnamon and bananas and beat well. Stir in remaining ingredients. Lightly spray a 9-x-13-inch pan with nonstick cooking spray. Spread mixture evenly into pan. Bake at 350° for 50 minutes. Cool and cut into bars. Makes 12 bars.

---

***per bar*** *298 calories, 8 g protein, 39 g carbo., 14 g fat, 40% calories from fat*

# APPLENUTTIES

*These cookies freeze well if they aren't all eaten first.*

1 cup apple butter
½ cup peanut butter
1 tsp. vanilla extract
¾ cup instant nonfat dry milk

¾ cup flour
¼ tsp. cinnamon
½ cup raisins

Beat apple butter, peanut butter and vanilla together in a bowl. Add dry milk, flour, cinnamon and raisins. Mix well. Drop by teaspoonfuls onto a greased cookie sheet. Flatten with the tines of a fork. Bake at 350° for 10 minutes. Serve warm or chilled. Makes 30 cookies.

*per cookie   68 calories, 2.1 g protein, 10.5 g carbo., 2.3 g fat, 29% calories from fat*

# PETER COTTONTAILS

*The kids will enjoy helping you make these.*

1 pkg. (3 oz.) nonfat cream cheese
½ cup shredded cheddar cheese
1 cup finely shredded carrots
½ cup Grape Nuts cereal

Beat cheeses together until blended. Stir in carrots. Cover and chill. Shape into balls, roll in cereal and chill until ready to serve. Makes 16 balls.

***per ball*** *36 calories, 2 g protein, 4.5 g carbo., 1.2 g fat, 30% calories from fat*

# BAKED VEGGIE SPREAD

*Serve this spread cold with toasted bread or rye crackers. It's a sneaky way to get kids to eat their veggies.*

1 eggplant, unpeeled
2 carrots
1 pkg. (10 oz.) French-cut green beans
3 small zucchini
¾ cup ketchup
1 can (8 oz.) tomato sauce
1 tbs. olive oil

Chop eggplant, carrots, beans and zucchini and place in a baking dish. Combine ketchup, tomato sauce and oil. Pour over veggies. Bake, covered, at 325° for 1½ hours. Serve cold. Makes 6 cups.

---

**per ½ cup**   *50 calories, 1.3 g protein, 9.7 g carbo., 1.3 g fat, 21% calories from fat*

# ZIPPETY DIPS

*Dips are a great way for kids to eat vegetables, fruit and other nutritious foods. Unless otherwise stated, veggie dippers can be raw or cooked. Raw vegetables have more nutrients than their cooked counterparts.*

## Veggie Dippers

- cooked artichokes
- asparagus spears
- cooked baby red potatoes
- broccoli florets
- carrot sticks
- cauliflower florets
- celery sticks
- cherry tomatoes
- cucumber rounds
- fennel strips

- raw mushrooms
- bell pepper strips
- jicama slices
- pickles
- radishes
- cooked turnip strips
- yam or sweet potato strips
- yellow squash slices
- zucchini strips

## Fruit Dippers

- apple wedges
- bananas
- melon slices
- grapes
- Mandarin orange segments

- melon slices
- pear wedges
- pineapple slices
- strawberries

## Other Dippers

- breadsticks
- chicken strips
- gingersnaps
- low salt tortilla chips
- whole wheat crackers
- crispy pita wedges

- toasted French bread rounds
- toast shapes
- pretzels
- cooked shrimp
- canned water chestnuts

# CUCUMBER DIP

*Add fresh chopped dill and this dip tastes like a pickle!*

8 oz. yogurt cheese or nonfat cream cheese
½ cup peeled chopped cucumber
2 tbs. lemon juice
½ tbs. mustard

Combine all ingredients in a blender container and whirl until smooth. Makes 1½ cups.

---

*per ¼ cup*  49 calories, 4.6 g protein, 7.4 g carbo., 0.2 g fat, 4% calories from fat

# CHILI DIP

*Kidney beans are a good source of vitamin A, protein and fiber.*

1 can (16 oz.) kidney beans, drained
1 tbs. vinegar
¾ tsp. chili powder
¼ tsp. salt
1 tbs. minced onion
1 tsp. dried parsley

Combine all ingredients in a blender container and whirl until smooth. Makes 1½ cups.

*per ¼ cup   66 calories, 24.1 g protein, 73.5 g carbo., 1.9 g fat, 4% calories from fat*

# COTTAGE CHEESE DIP

*This calcium-rich dip will appeal to even the most die-hard milk hater.*

1 cup plain nonfat yogurt
1 cup low fat cottage cheese
1/4 cup grated Parmesan cheese
1/4 cup canned artichoke hearts, drained

Combine all ingredients in a blender container and whirl until smooth. Makes 2 1/2 cups.

*per 1/4 cup*   *48 calories, 5.4 g protein, 3 g carbo., 2 g fat, 29% calories from fat*

# FRUIT DIP

*This dip makes a good milkshake when blended with a little cold nonfat (skim) milk. Use the kids' favorite fruit.*

1 cup plain nonfat yogurt
½ cup chopped fruit

Combine all ingredients in a blender container and whirl until smooth. Makes 1½ cups.

*per ¼ cup   31 calories, 2.3 g protein, 5.6 g carbo., 0.1 g fat, 2% calories from fat*

# DYNAMITE DRINKS

# PACK YOUR PUNCH WITH POWER

It's amazing what you can sneak into a drink and get away with! As long as you blend the ingredients well in a blender and serve them chilled, your child will never suspect what's making the drink taste so delicious. You can even provide a complete meal in one glass. Add extra fruit, vegetables or wheat germ to anything you're preparing for your child. The idea is to pack as much good nutrition as possible into whatever your child is eating and drinking. Anytime you can add a little something extra, do it!

Serve drinks in a way that will be especially appealing to your child. Buy some new mugs with his or her favorite characters on them to use when you offer a new drink. Or serve it in one of your special champagne or wine glasses as an added treat. Scooped-out orange shells are another way to dress up a drink and you don't have to wash the glass! Children love "crazy" straws that look like complex freeway overpasses. It's great fun to watch the different colored beverages flow through.

# FOUR-FRUIT FLOAT

*So refreshing! Use fresh or frozen berries.*

½ cup sliced strawberries
½ cup raspberries
½ cup blueberries
½ cup 2% milk
1 cup apple juice

Combine ingredients in a blender container. Blend until smooth. Makes 2 to 4 servings.

*per serving*   *67 calories, 1.4 g protein, 14.4 g carbo., 0.9 g fat, 11% calories from fat*

# MONKEY MILKSHAKE

*This is a meal in a glass. Even those who don't like milk will ask for more.*

1 cup sliced strawberries
1 banana
1 cup nonfat (skim) milk
2 tsp. vanilla extract
3 ice cubes

Combine ingredients in a blender container. Blend until smooth and fluffy. Makes 2 to 3 servings.

*per serving*   117 calories, 5.2 g protein, 24.6 g carbo., 0.8 g fat, 5% calories from fat

# V-3 JUICE

*It's worth a try, isn't it?*

¼ cup chopped celery
¼ cup coarsely grated peeled carrot
¼ cup any other vegetable
1 cup tomato juice

Combine ingredients in a blender container. Blend until smooth. Serve immediately or chill before serving. Makes 2 servings.

*per serving*   *35 calories, 1.3 g protein, 8.5 g carbo., 0.1 g fat, 3% calories from fat*

# ORANGE PLUS TWO

*Here's a pleasant change from the usual morning glass of orange juice.*

1 cup orange juice
1 cup cranberry juice cocktail
1 cup club soda
ice to fill glasses

Mix orange juice, cranberry juice and soda together in a pitcher. Pour juice over ice in serving glasses. Makes 2 to 4 servings.

*per serving*   *126 calories, 1 g protein, 30.6 g carbo., 0.5 g fat, 3% calories from fat*

# SIMPLE SIMON CIDER

*Perfect for a cold winter evening or in the lunch box vacuum bottle.*

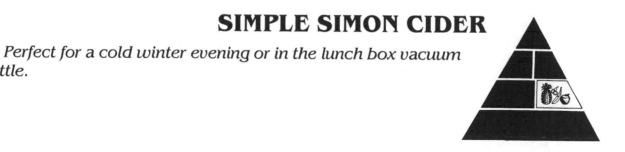

3 cinnamon sticks
1 bottle (46 oz.) natural apple juice
1 can (11.5 oz.) apricot nectar

Bring ingredients to a boil in a large saucepan. Simmer for 10 minutes. Serve warm. Makes 6 to 8 servings.

*per serving*   133 calories, 0.3 g protein, 33.6 g carbo., 0.3 g fat, 2% calories from fat

# FRUIT FIZZIE

*For variety, use apple or grape juice. Fruit nectar can be sub-
stituted by mixing it with equal parts water.*

1 can (6 oz.) frozen orange juice concentrate
4 bottles (10 oz. each) sparkling mineral water

Combine ingredients. Serve in frosty glasses. Makes 4 to 6 servings.

*per serving*   68 calories, 1 g protein, 16.2 g carbo., 0.1 g fat, 1% calories from fat

# FRUIT JUICIE

*Makes enough for the whole neighborhood.*

1 pt. strawberries
2 tbs. lemon juice
3 cups boiling water
3 cups cold water
½ cup orange juice
crushed ice

Combine ½ of the strawberries, lemon juice and boiling water in a blender container. Blend until smooth. Pour into a large bowl or pitcher. Repeat process with remaining strawberries, lemon juice and boiling water and add to first mixture. Stir in cold water and orange juice. Chill. Serve over crushed ice. Makes 8 to 10 servings.

***per serving***   *25 calories, 0.5 g protein, 5.9 g carbo., 0.3 g fat, 8% calories from fat*

# GRAHAM CRACKER FOAMY

*This makes a good breakfast drink.*

1½ cups 2% milk
2 graham crackers, broken
½ tsp. honey, if desired
2 tbs. frozen orange juice concentrate

Combine ingredients in a blender container. Blend until smooth and frothy. Makes 2 servings.

***per serving***   *152 calories, 7.1 g protein, 22.2 g carbo., 4.2 g fat, 24% calories from fat*

# SURPRISE SHAKE

*You can't taste the wheat germ, yet it adds so much!*

6 tbs. frozen orange juice concentrate
1 cup 2% milk
2 tsp. wheat germ
3 ice cubes

Combine ingredients in a blender container. Blend until frothy. Makes 2 servings.

*per serving   153 calories, 5.8 g protein, 27.3 g carbo., 2.7 g fat, 15% calories from fat*

# MIGHTY MILK

*Buttermilk, despite its name, does not contain any butter. It's actually 1% low fat milk with the addition of beneficial bacteria as you would find in yogurt. Although it has a slightly sour taste that many kids don't like, this recipe disguises it. Honestly, you can't taste the buttermilk!*

1 can (6 oz.) frozen orange juice concentrate
2 cups buttermilk
1 tsp. honey

Combine ingredients in a blender container. Blend until frothy. Serve over ice. Makes 2 to 4 servings.

*per serving*    *245 calories, 10.2 g protein, 47.1 g carbo., 2.3 g fat, 8% calories from fat*

# FRUITY LEMONADE

*You can substitute 1 qt. lemonade made from frozen concentrate for the first 3 ingredients if you prefer. Use raspberries, blackberries, boysenberries and/or chopped strawberries.*

2 large lemons
½ cup honey, or to taste
3½ cups water
1 cup fresh berries or thawed frozen berries

Squeeze lemons through a strainer into a large bowl. Stir in honey gradually to taste. Add water and berries. Pour into glasses and serve. Makes 4 to 6 servings.

***per serving*** *148 calories, 0.7 g protein, 40 g carbo., 0.2 g fat, 1% calories from fat*

# JERSEY JUICE

*Juice and milk? It's surprisingly good!*

1 can (6 oz.) frozen orange juice concentrate
2½ cups 2% milk

Combine ingredients in a blender container. Blend until frothy. Makes 3 to 4 servings.

*per serving*   *191 calories, 8.1 g protein, 30.4 g carbo., 4 g fat, 19% calories from fat*

# ORANGE JUBILEE

*Make plain orange juice elegant and extra-nutritious. Add a little water if the blender won't turn.*

1 can (6 oz.) orange juice concentrate
⅓ cup instant nonfat dry milk
½ tsp. vanilla extract
ice cubes to fill blender

Place orange juice concentrate into a blender container. Add instant milk and blend until mixed. Add vanilla extract and ice cubes and blend on high speed until smooth. Makes 2 servings.

---

***per serving***   *176 calories, 6 g protein, 38.4 g carbo., 0.3 fat, 1% calories from fat*

# NEW YORK "EGG CREAM"

*Only in New York would a drink called Egg Cream be made without eggs or cream. A legend! Serve with **Hot Cheese Funnies**, page 36.*

1 cup club soda
1 cup 2% milk
1 tbs. chocolate syrup or 1 tsp. each carob powder and honey

   Combine ingredients in a blender container. Blend on high speed until frothy. Makes 2 servings.

***per serving***   *81 calories, 4.2 g protein, 11.4 g carbo., 2.4 g fat, 26% calories from fat*

# BOYSENBERRY BLITZ

*This is very refreshing on a warm day. Serve in frosty glasses.*

1 cup 2% milk
1 carton (8 oz.) boysenberry low fat yogurt

Combine ingredients in a blender container. Blend until frothy. Makes 2 servings.

***per serving*** *176 calories, 9 g protein, 27.5 g carbo., 3.6 g fat, 18% calories form fat*

## VARIATION: BOYSENBERRY MILKSHAKE

Combine 1 cup frozen boysenberries, 1 cup vanilla ice milk and ¼ cup 2% milk in a blender container. Blend until smooth. Makes 2 servings.

***per serving*** *135 calories, 4.4 g protein, 24 g carbo., 3 g fat, 19% calories from fat*

# FLORIDA FROSTY

*This tastes especially good on a hot day.*

1 cup orange juice
½ cup plain low fat yogurt
1 banana

    Combine ingredients in blender container. Blend until smooth. Serve immediately in frosty cold glasses. Makes 2 servings.

*per serving*   *143 calories, 4.6 g protein, 29.9 g carbo., 1.5 g fat, 9% calories from fat*

# MOOSEBERRY JUICE

*Sneak in a little wheat germ any time you can!*

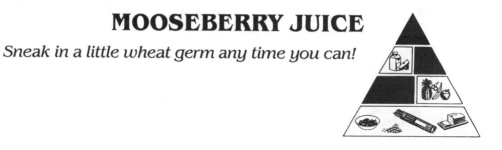

1 pkg. (10 oz.) frozen raspberries
1½ cups 2% milk
1 tbs. wheat germ

Combine ingredients in a blender container. Blend until smooth. Makes 3 to 4 servings.

*per serving   165 calories, 5.2 g protein, 31.6 g carbo., 2.7 g fat, 14% calories from fat*

# FRUIT FRAPPÉ

*Use berries, peaches, apricots, pears or melon for this Italian favorite.*

⅔ cup 2% milk
⅔ cup fresh fruit, cut into pieces
1 tsp. honey, if desired
¼ cup crushed ice

Combine ingredients in a blender container. Blend on high speed until smooth and frothy. Makes 2 servings.

*per serving*   *70 calories, 3 g protein, 11.6 g carbo., 1.6 g fat, 20% calories from fat*

# BLENDER BERRIES

*Choose your favorite: strawberries, blueberries or boysenberries.*

½ cup plain nonfat yogurt
2 tbs. water
1 cup fresh or frozen berries
1 banana
1 tbs. wheat germ
⅛ tsp. cinnamon
¼ tsp. lemon juice

Combine ingredients in a blender container. Blend until smooth. Serve chilled in frosty glasses. Makes 2 servings.

***per serving***   *126 calories, 4.6 g protein, 25.6 g carbo., 1.6 g fat, 10% calories from fat*

# PEACH FUZZ

*Many of the canned fruits today are available without added sugar. Look for labels that say "lite," "natural," or "packed in its own juice." Some have added no extra sugar and others have reduced the amount by 50%. You can substitute 2 peeled ripe peaches for canned peaches when they're in season.*

1 banana
3 canned peach halves
2 cups 2% milk
½ tsp. vanilla extract
1 carton (8 oz.) plain low fat yogurt
5 ice cubes

Combine all ingredients in a blender container. Blend until smooth and frothy. Makes 4 to 6 servings.

*per serving*   *564 calories, 7.6 g protein, 21.4 g carbo., 3.4 g fat, 21% calories from fat*

# BREAKFAST SHAKE

*No time to cook breakfast? Try this as a morning meal with some whole grain toast.*

2 cups nonfat (skim) milk
1/2 cup plain low fat yogurt
1 tbs. vanilla extract
2 tsp. nutmeg
1 cup instant nonfat dry milk
1 banana
1 can (6 oz.) frozen orange juice concentrate

Place all ingredients in a blender container. Blend until frothy. Makes 4 servings.

***per serving*** *221 calories, 13 g protein, 40.3 g carbo., 1.4 g fat, 6% calories from fat*

# APPLE SHAKE

*Substitute different fruit juices for variety.*

1 cup vanilla ice milk
½ cup apple juice
¼ tsp. cinnamon

Place all ingredients in a blender container. Blend until smooth and frothy. Makes 2 servings.

***per serving*** *121 calories, 2.6 g protein, 22 g carbo., 2.9 g fat, 21% calories from fat*

# FROSTY FRUIT FLOAT

*It doesn't take much ice milk to make this drink special. Use orange, grape, cranberry, pineapple or another favorite fruit juice.*

¼ cup fruit juice
1 tbs. vanilla ice milk
1 bottle (10 oz.) club soda

Pour juice into a tall glass. Add ice milk. Fill with club soda. Stir and serve. Makes 2 servings.

*per serving   19 calories, 0.4 g protein, 4 g carbo., 0.3 g fat, 12% calories from fat*

# HAWAIIAN SHAKE

*Substitute fresh pineapple for the canned variety when you find it in the market. Process it for a few seconds in a food processor or blender to "crush."*

2 cups crushed pineapple
2 cups nonfat (skim) milk
1 pt. vanilla ice milk
1 tbs. lemon juice

Combine ingredients in a blender container. Blend until smooth. Makes 6 to 8 servings.

---

***per serving*** *153 calories, 4.8 g protein, 26.8 g carbo., 3.5 g fat, 20% calories from fat*

# BANANA SMOOTHY

*Make a bet with your child that she or he can drink a whole banana.*

1½ cups 2% milk
1 large banana
¼ tsp. vanilla extract
¼ cup vanilla ice milk

Combine ingredients in a blender container. Blend until smooth and creamy. Makes 2 servings.

*per serving*   *166 calories, 7.4 g protein, 25.6 g carbo., 4.5 g fat, 23% calories from fat*

# BANANA CHOCOLATE FROTH

*This potassium-packed shake tastes deceivingly rich.*

1 cup 2% milk
1 banana
¾ cup vanilla ice milk
2 tbs. cocoa powder

Combine ingredients in a blender container. Blend until smooth and creamy. Makes 2 servings.

*per serving*   *188 calories, 7.1 g protein, 31.4 g carbo., 5.2 g fat, 23% calories from fat*

# GRAPE SLUSH

*This shake tastes like liquid sherbet; a favorite!*

¼ cup frozen grape juice concentrate
¼ cup frozen orange juice concentrate
½ cup 2% milk
½ cup vanilla ice milk
1 banana

Combine all ingredients in a blender container. Blend until smooth. Serve in icy cold glasses. Makes 2 servings.

*per serving*   249 calories, 5 g protein, 53 g carbo., 3 g fat, 11% calories from fat

# BANORBERRY SMOOTHY

*This thick drink gives your child a head start on the food pyramid's fruit group. Garnish glasses with an orange slice and a crazy curly straw.*

1 cup strawberries
1 banana
1 cup orange juice

Place all ingredients in a blender container and process until smooth. Makes 2 to 3 servings.

*per serving*   *130 calories, 1.9 g protein, 31.5 g carbo., 0.8 g fat, 5% calories from fat*

# FROZEN FUN

# PUT YOUR LOCAL ICE CREAM TRUCK
# OUT OF BUSINESS

Frozen snacks are extremely popular with kids all year long. They are a great way to disguise unpopular fruits and vegetables. (Your child doesn't have to know how *Rabbit Sherbet* got its name.) Sugar should be kept to a minimum in a child's diet, but it doesn't have to be avoided altogether. A little jam for flavor, or sherbet or ice milk, combined with other nutritious ingredients, can become a special frozen treat that most children are sure to eat.

The main object of all the recipes in this book is to help you make your child's diet as healthy as possible. Since snacks are a big part of that diet, they are a great vehicle for packing healthy foods into favorites a child will eat. The snacks in this chapter are easy to make, taste great and are a whole lot more nutritious than the frozen "colored sugar water" you can buy at the supermarket. They are probably a lot less expensive, too.

If you don't have popsicle molds, keep on hand a supply of popsicle sticks, empty juice cans and 5 or 9 oz. paper "dixie" cups to make homemade popsicles. If using cans, dip them briefly in hot water to loosen the frozen snack. Paper cups can simply be peeled away and discarded.

# FROZEN BANANAS

*Serve these on a high activity day for a quick energy boost. Reduced fat peanut butter can be used to lower the fat percentage. Cut these into small chips for the young ones.*

2 bananas
½ cup peanut butter
½ cup wheat germ

Peel bananas and cut in half crosswise. Insert a popsicle stick into the flat end of each banana. Wrap bananas in plastic wrap and freeze. When frozen, place peanut butter and wheat germ into separate bowls. Dip bananas into peanut butter and then into wheat germ and serve. Makes 4 servings.

***per serving***   *291 calories, 10.1 g protein, 31.6 g carbo., 16.3 g fat, 47% calories from fat*

# ESKIMO FRUIT

*Sometimes just making it cold makes fruit taste better! Put one or more of the following items in the freezer for a refreshing treat. Or, make up your own frozen fun!*

- apples
- apricots
- bananas
- blueberries
- cantaloupe
- cherries
- dried fruits
- fruit leather
- gelatin snacks
- grapefruit
- grapes

- kiwi
- mangoes
- oranges
- papayas
- peaches
- pineapple
- plums
- raisins
- raspberries
- strawberries
- watermelon

# KING KONG'S CHIPS

*These treats take only minutes and the kids can help.*

2 bananas, sliced
½ cup orange juice
½ cup wheat germ

Dip banana slices into orange juice then into wheat germ. Arrange in cake pans or on plates in a single layer. Cover with plastic and freeze. Makes 4 servings.

---

***per serving*** *111 calories, 3.7 g protein, 23 g carbo., 1.6 g fat, 12% calories from fat*

# FROSTBITE BLIZZARD

*The kids will think they've gone to the fair for snow cones, but their lips won't be stained blue.*

ice cubes
fruit nectar, fruit juice or fruit puree

Crush ice in a heavy plastic bag with a hammer or use a blender or food processor to make "snow." Scoop into a bowl. Pour fruit juice or puree over snow and serve with a spoon.

*per cup fruit nectar*  *140 calories, 0.9 g protein, 36.1 g carbo., 0 g fat, 0% calories from fat*

# WIGGLE SICLES

*You can substitute packaged gelatin or pudding for unflavored gelatin and fruit puree, but those products are high in refined sugar. The protein in this recipe comes from the gelatin.*

1 pkg. (¼ oz.) unflavored gelatin
¾ cup boiling water
½ cup fruit puree (strawberry, plum, peach, etc.)

Dissolve gelatin in boiling water. Add fruit puree. Stir until well blended and pour into paper cups. Cover cups with foil. Make a slit in the center of each foil cover. Insert sticks and freeze. Makes 2 servings.

---

**per serving**   *45 calories, 3.2 g protein, 8.7 g carbo., 0 g fat, 0% calories from fat*

# BANANA FROSTEE

*Vanilla extract is the secret ingredient in this recipe. It adds an extra flavor dimension that your kids will love.*

¼ cup apple juice
2 bananas, sliced and frozen
1 tsp. vanilla extract
½ cup chilled sliced peaches or strawberries

Combine juice and bananas in a blender container. Blend until creamy. Quickly blend in chilled fruit. Serve immediately. Makes 2 servings.

*per serving*   *130 calories, 1.4 g protein, 33 g carbo., 0.7 g fat, 4% calories from fat*

# BANAPPLE BARS

*Here's a popsicle with the taste of the tropics.*

1 cup pineapple juice
1 banana

Combine juice and banana in a blender container. Blend on high speed until smooth. Pour into paper cups. Cover cups with foil. Make a slit in the center of each foil cover. Insert popsicle sticks. Freeze. Makes 2 servings.

*per serving*   *117 calories, 1.1 g protein, 29.3 g carbo., 0.3 g fat, 2% calories from fat*

# TROPICAL POPS

*Ask the kids to guess what flavor these are. Odds are they won't figure it out.*

1 apple, peeled and chopped
1 orange, peeled and sectioned
1 banana, peeled and sliced
½ cup sliced pineapple, fresh or canned
1 pear, peeled and chopped
1 cup frozen strawberries with juice

Combine all ingredients in a blender container and puree. Pour into paper cups. Cover cups with foil. Make a slit in the center of each foil cover. Insert popsicle sticks and freeze. Makes 4 to 6 servings.

---

***per serving*** *109 calories, 1.1 g protein, 27.8 g carbo., 0.6 g fat, 4% calories from fat*

# ARCTIC ORANGES

*Save these for a special occasion. Garnish with a little yogurt and a cherry. Mom: add 3 tbs. Grand Marnier to the mixture and serve them at your next dinner party!*

3 oranges
¼ cup honey, or to taste
½ cup water
1 tbs. lemon juice

Using a zigzag pattern, cut tops off oranges. Hollow out and reserve fruit. Set orange shells in muffin cups so they won't topple over. Squeeze and strain orange juice. Set aside. Cook honey and water in a small saucepan over low heat until slightly thickened, about 15 minutes. Add orange juice and lemon juice to mixture. Fill oranges and freeze. Makes 6 servings.

---

***per serving***   *74 calories, 0.7 g protein, 19.5 g carbo., 0.1 g fat, 1% calories from fat*

# HAWAIIAN ICE

*Peaches can be substituted for nectarines.*

4 nectarines, cubed
2 bananas, sliced
juice of 2 oranges

juice of 2 lemons
1 can (8 oz.) crushed pineapple
½ cup water

Combine nectarines and bananas in a blender container. Blend until smooth. Add orange juice, lemon juice, pineapple and water. Blend until smooth. Pour into a large container. Cover and freeze. When ready to serve, let stand at room temperature for about 20 minutes. Scoop into individual dishes. Makes 6 to 8 servings.

*per serving*   *128 calories, 2 g protein, 32.5 g carbo., 0.7 g fat, 5% calories from fat*

# FROZEN JAMMIES

*Combining these unusual ingredients yields a surprisingly delicious frozen treat.*

3 cups buttermilk
2 cups strawberry or plum jam

Beat ingredients together until blended. Pour into ice cube trays and freeze until firm. Release cubes from tray and beat with an electric mixer until fluffy. Spoon into individual containers and return to freezer until ready to serve. Makes 4 to 6 servings.

*per serving*   *510 calories, 7.1 g protein, 120.8 g carbo., 1.8 g fat, 3% calories from fat*

# FRUIT SHERBIES

*Don't mention the word buttermilk and they'll ask for more.*

1 can (6 oz.) frozen orange juice concentrate
3 cans water
2 cups fruit puree or nectar
⅔ cup buttermilk

Combine ingredients. Pour into paper cups. Cover cups with foil. Make a small slit in the center of each cover. Insert popsicle sticks and freeze. Makes 4 to 6 servings.

*per serving*   *151 calories, 2.7 g protein, 35.5 g carbo., 0.5 g fat, 3% calories from fat*

# GELLAPOPS

*These are much more nutritious than commercial popsicles. Apple or grape juice concentrate make nice variations. Gelatin adds protein to these jiggly popsicles.*

1½ pkg. (¼ oz. each) unflavored gelatin
¾ cup boiling water
1 can (6 oz.) frozen orange juice concentrate
2 cups cold water
1 carton (32 oz.) plain low fat yogurt

Dissolve gelatin in boiling water in a large bowl. Add juice concentrate and cold water. Add yogurt and stir until blended. Pour into paper cups. Cover cups with foil. Make a small slit in the center of each foil cover. Insert popsicle sticks and freeze. Makes 6 to 8 servings.

*per serving* *146 calories, 10.1 g protein, 21.5 g carbo., 2.4 g fat, 15% calories from fat*

# CHOCKSICLES

*Appease your chocolate lovers with this low fat treat.*

1 cup plain low fat yogurt
2 tbs. cocoa powder
1 tsp. honey

Blend ingredients and pour into paper cups. Cover cups with foil. Make a small slit in the center of each foil cover. Insert sticks and freeze. Makes 2 servings.

*per serving*   *96 calories, 6.9 g protein, 13.5 g carbo., 2.8 g fat, 23% calories from fat*

# PIZZAZZ POPS

*Fizzy soda makes these popsicles extra special.*

1 cup evaporated milk
1 bottle (28 oz.) flavored soda
½ cup lemon juice

Mix all ingredients well. Pour into paper cups. Cover cups with foil. Make a small slit in the center of each foil cover. Insert popsicle sticks and freeze. Makes 4 to 6 servings.

*per serving*   *183 calories, 4.4 g protein, 31.3 g carbo., 4.8 g fat, 23% calories from fat*

# RABBIT SHERBET

*This snack is devious, but delicious. Carrots are an important source of vitamins.*

1 cup sliced cooked carrots
¼ cup orange juice
1 pt. orange sherbet, softened

Combine carrots and orange juice in a blender container. Blend until smooth. Fold into softened sherbet. Pour into a large plastic container or bowl. Cover and freeze. Scoop sherbet into individual cups to serve. Makes 3 to 4 servings.

*per serving*   *205 calories, 2 g protein, 45 g carbo., 2.7 g fat, 11% calories from fat*

# CINNAMON SICLES

*Eating these is just like eating frozen apple pie.*

1 cup plain low fat yogurt
1 cup applesauce
½ tsp. cinnamon
1 tbs. honey, if desired

Blend yogurt, applesauce, cinnamon and honey, if using. Pour into paper cups. Cover cups with foil. Make a slit in the center of each foil cover and insert popsicle sticks. Freeze. Makes 2 to 3 servings.

*per serving*   *157 calories, 6.2 g protein, 30.9 g carbo., 1.8 g fat, 10% calories from fat*

# FROZEN YOGGIES

*It is possible to make your own frozen yogurt pops, and yours won't have additives or preservatives.*

1 cup orange juice
2 cups plain low fat yogurt
1 tsp. vanilla extract

Combine juice, yogurt and vanilla extract. Pour into paper cups. Cover cups with foil. Make a slit in the center of each foil cover and insert popsicle sticks. Freeze until firm. Makes 3 to 4 servings.

*per serving*   *133 calories, 8.5 g protein, 19.6 g carbo., 2.4 g fat, 16% calories from fat.*

# HULA POPS

*These taste perfect after a long day at the beach. Use apricots, strawberries, peaches, nectarines, pineapple or a combination for the fruit.*

1 cup plain low fat yogurt
1 banana
1 tsp. honey, if desired
½ cup orange or pineapple juice
1 cup sliced fruit

Combine ingredients in a blender container. Blend on high speed until smooth. Pour into paper cups. Cover cups with foil. Make a slit in the center of each foil cover. Insert sticks and freeze. Makes 6 to 8 servings.

*per serving*   *61 calories, 2.5 g protein, 11.9 g carbo., 0.8 g fat, 11% calories from fat*

# PEACHERITOS

*Experiment with strawberries or bananas too.*

1 can (28 oz.) peaches or 3 fresh peaches, peeled and sliced
1½ cups 2% milk

Combine ingredients in a blender container. Blend until smooth. Pour into paper cups. Cover cups with foil. Make a small slit in the center of each foil cover. Insert popsicle sticks and freeze. Makes 4 to 6 servings.

*per serving*   *74 calories, 3.5 g protein, 11.6 g carbo., 1.8 g fat, 21% calories from fat*

# FREEZE YOUR FAVORITES

Almost anything tastes better to kids when it is frozen. Pour your child's favorite drink into popsicle molds and watch his or her face light up with excitement. Choose any of the following drinks from the **Dynamite Drinks** chapter or make up your own recipe.

- *Four-Fruit Float*, page 55
- *Orange Plus Two*, page 58
- *Fruit Fizzie*, page 60
- *Fruit Juicie*, page 61
- *Mighty Milk*, page 64
- *Fruity Lemonade*, page 65
- *Jersey Juice*, page 66
- *New York "Egg Cream,"* page 68
- *Boysenberry Blitz*, page 69
- *Boysenberry Milkshake*, page 69
- *Florida Frosty*, page 70
- *Breakfast Shake*, page 75
- *Hawaiian Shake*, page 78
- *Banana Smoothy*, page 79
- *Banorberry Smoothy*, page 82

# ICED TEASERS

*Herbal tea is refreshing and light to drink on a hot summer day, but it's even more fun frozen. Toss bits of fruit into the popsicle cup for garnish.*

3 cups brewed herbal tea, such as lemon or berry
3 cups orange juice

Blend ingredients. Pour into paper cups or popsicle molds. Cover cups with foil. Make a small slit in the center of each foil cover. Insert popsicle sticks and freeze. Makes 6 to 8 servings.

***per serving*** *57 calories, 0.9 g protein, 13.1 g carbo., 0.3 g fat, 4% calories from fat*

# WATERMELON WANNABES

*Watermelon is rich in vitamins A and C, and kids love it. The carob chips resemble seeds, but they taste much better.*

2 cups chopped seeded watermelon
1 cup apple juice
½ cup carob chips

Combine watermelon and apple juice in a blender container. Blend until smooth. Pour into a freezer-proof bowl and freeze until semi-solid. Stir in carob chips. Carefully spoon mixture into paper cups. Cover cups with foil. Make a small slit in the center of each foil cover. Insert popsicle sticks and freeze until solid. Makes 6 to 8 servings.

---

***per serving*** *83 calories, 0.4 g protein, 13.8 g carbo., 2.4 g fat, 29% calories from fat*

# BETTER BREAKFASTS

# MAKE SENSE OF MORNING MADNESS

Are you stuck in the bacon-and-egg or cereal rut? Take a look at the recipes in this chapter and you'll see that your dilemma is resolved. There are many wonderful alternatives that children love.

Now you can be creative and still provide a wholesome breakfast in minutes. Many recipes can be made the evening before, or on weekends and then frozen. All you have to do on those rushed, early mornings is heat the treat-of-the-day in a microwave, conventional oven or in the toaster. You can mix and match with recipes from other chapters in the book for more variety.

Many authorities recommend that children over the age of 2 eat no more than 30% of their daily calories in the form of fat. If some of the dishes here appear high in fat, average that number into the total number of calories in that meal, including the orange juice and garnishes. Also, remember that the guidelines are for TOTAL DAILY CALORIES. It's OK to indulge at one meal as long as you moderate fat intake throughout the rest of the day.

# FRISKY FRITTATA

*Half pizza, half quiche, but all delicious!*

1 egg
¾ cup flour
½ tsp. salt
¼ tsp. dried oregano

1 cup 2% milk
1 cup grated part-skim mozzarella
  cheese
3 tbs. grated Parmesan cheese

Mix egg with flour, salt, oregano and milk. Pour into a blender container and whirl until foamy. Add mozzarella cheese and pour into a greased pie pan. Bake at 400° for 30 minutes. Top with Parmesan cheese. Broil briefly until Parmesan is slightly melted. Serve warm or cold. Makes 6 servings.

*per serving*   *157 calories, 10.5 g protein, 14.7 g carbo., 5.9 g fat, 35% calories from fat*

# HOT CEREAL SURPRISE

*Mikey won't eat his Maypo? Try this little surprise.*

1 cup cooked oatmeal
1 apple, chopped
1 cup 2% milk
1-2 tbs. honey, if desired
¼ cup raisins, chopped dried apricots or dates
¼ tsp. cinnamon

Combine cooked cereal, apple, milk, honey, if using, fruit and cinnamon in a saucepan. Cook over low heat for 5 to 10 minutes. Serve hot. Makes 2 servings.

*per serving* *277 calories, 7.9 g protein, 56.5 g carbo., 3.9 g fat, 12% calories from fat*

# MACARONI OMELET

*By using egg substitute instead of eggs, you can reduce the fat in this recipe from 41% to 31%. Use ¼ cup liquid egg substitute for each large egg. Serve this omelet in scooped-out orange halves for a fresh look.*

2 eggs, beaten
1 cup chopped cooked broccoli
½ cup cooked macaroni
¼ cup grated Parmesan cheese

Mix eggs with broccoli and macaroni. Scramble in a nonstick skillet until fluffy. Sprinkle with Parmesan cheese. Makes 2 servings.

***per serving*** *203 calories, 15.5 g protein, 15 g carbo., 9.3 g fat, 41% calories from fat*

# NUTTY FRUITY TOAST

*This recipe puts a whole breakfast on a slice of toast. If desired, substitute dried apricots for the raisins. Reduced fat peanut butter and egg substitute will lower the fat percentage.*

3 tbs. peanut butter
¼ cup chopped raisins
2 tbs. jam
1 tsp. cinnamon

4 slices whole wheat bread
1 egg
¼ cup nonfat (skim) milk
1 tbs. margarine

Combine peanut butter, raisins, jam and cinnamon. Spread mixture on 2 slices of the bread. Top with remaining bread slices to form a sandwich. In a pie plate or shallow bowl, beat eggs and stir in milk. Dip each sandwich in egg mixture. Melt margarine in a skillet. Brown sandwiches on both sides. Makes 2 servings.

*per serving*  *479 calories, 16.9 g protein, 61.3 g carbo., 21.5 g fat, 38% calories from fat*

# SQUARE MEAL SQUARES

*Here's another complete-meal-on-toast.*

1 cup low fat cottage cheese
1 tbs. honey, if desired
½ cup chopped walnuts
2 slices whole wheat toast or waffle squares
1 banana, sliced
2 tsp. wheat germ

Combine cottage cheese, honey, if using, and nuts. Spread on toast. Top with banana slices and sprinkle with wheat germ. Makes 2 servings.

*per serving*   223 calories, 20.2 g protein, 41.6 g carbo., 12.1 g fat, 31% calories from fat

# SWEET BREAD

*This will make a "breakfast eater" out of everyone. Prepare the cheese mixture the night before. Substitute English muffins for variety.*

1 cup low fat cottage cheese
¼ cup chopped dates or prunes
¼ cup chopped walnuts
1 tsp. honey, if desired
½ tsp. cinnamon
2 slices whole wheat bread

Mix cheese, dates, nuts, honey, if using, and cinnamon together. Store in the refrigerator. When ready to serve, spread mixture on bread slices. Broil until bubbly. Makes 2 servings.

*per serving* *356 calories, 21.8 g protein, 43.1 g carbo., 12.6 g fat, 30% calories from fat*

# CHEESY BREAKFAST SANDWICH

*This one's yummy served warm or cold.*

2 slices whole wheat bread
¼ cup chutney
2 slices turkey bacon, cooked
2 tbs. grated Parmesan cheese

Spread 1 slice of the bread with chutney. Top with bacon and cheese. Broil until cheese is melted. Cover with second bread slice. Makes 1 sandwich.

*per serving*   *278 calories, 13.4 g protein, 31.5 g carbo., 8.8 g fat, 28% calories from fat*

# FRUIT-N-CHEESE TOAST

*This is a wholesome American version of a Danish sweet roll. For variety, substitute a pear or banana for the apple.*

1 tbs. margarine
2 eggs
1 tbs. 2% milk
2 slices whole wheat bread

2 tbs. yogurt cheese or
    nonfat cream cheese
1 small apple, chopped
¼ tsp. lemon juice
2 tbs. raisins

Melt margarine in an 8-inch square baking pan in a 450° oven. Spread margarine evenly in pan. Separate 1 egg. Beat 1 whole egg and 1 egg white with milk. Dip bread in egg mixture, coating both sides. Place in pan. Bake for 5 minutes at 450°. Beat yogurt cheese and remaining egg yolk together. Mix apple, lemon juice and raisins. Remove bread from oven. Spread each slice with cheese mixture and top with fruit mixture. Bake for 5 minutes. Serve warm. Makes 2 servings.

*per serving*   *257 calories, 11.4 g protein, 30 g carbo., 11 g fat, 37% calories from fat*

# COCONUT TOASTIES

*Serve this as a special birthday breakfast surprise. Reduce the amount of coconut or use egg substitute if you're concerned about the fat percentage.*

2 eggs
½ cup 2% milk
½ cup crushed cornflakes
½ cup shredded unsweetened coconut

2 tbs. canola oil
8 slices whole wheat bread
1 can (8 oz.) crushed pineapple, warmed

Beat eggs with milk in a pie plate or shallow bowl. Combine cornflakes and coconut in another pie plate or shallow bowl. Heat margarine on a griddle over medium heat. Dip each slice of bread into egg mixture and then into coconut mixture, coating both sides. Cook on griddle until browned on both sides. Serve with warmed pineapple. Makes 4 servings.

*per serving*  *383 calories, 12.7 g protein, 48.9 g carbo., 17.2 g fat, 39% calories from fat*

# MAKE-BELIEVE WAFFLES

*Whole wheat bread makes good "waffles" when you don't have time to make your own. Pick a fresh fruit topping on page 125 to add more nutrients and reduce the amount of calories from fat.*

1 egg
¼ cup 2% milk
1 tbs. margarine, melted
2 slices whole wheat bread

Heat a waffle iron. Combine egg, milk and margarine in a pie plate or shallow bowl. Dip bread slices into mixture, one at a time, until well coated. Place bread in waffle iron and close cover. Cook until waffle iron stops steaming and opens easily. Makes 2 servings.

*per serving*   176 calories, 7.9 g protein, 18.5 g carbo., 8.5 g fat, 42% calories from fat

# BANANA FRANCAIS

*Fortify your French toast with potassium-rich banana slices and whole grain bread.*

2 eggs
1 banana, chopped
¼ cup 2% milk
½ tsp. cinnamon
2 tsp. canola oil
4 slices whole wheat bread

Combine eggs, banana, milk and cinnamon in a blender container. Blend until smooth. Pour into a pie plate. Soak bread in banana mixture. Heat oil in a large skillet until hot. Place bread in skillet. Spoon remaining banana mixture over each slice of bread. Cook over medium-high heat until brown on both sides. Makes 2 servings.

*per serving*  *352 calories, 15.2 g protein, 48.8 g carbo., 12.5 g fat, 31% calories from fat*

# INSTANT BRUNCH

*This "sandwich" is so fun to look at and delicious to eat, they won't know it's good for them. Use frozen waffles or make your own. If you make your own waffles, use part whole wheat flour and add up to ½ cup of wheat germ. Freeze the extras.*

2 tbs. yogurt cheese or nonfat cream cheese
2 tbs. strawberry jam
2 tbs. finely chopped walnuts
2 waffles, toasted

Mix cheese, jam and walnuts. Spread mixture on one of the waffles. Cover with second waffle. Cut into quarters and serve. Makes 2 servings.

*per serving*   *207 calories, 5.3 g protein, 32.3 g carbo., 6.9 g fat, 29% calories from fat*

# POTPOURRI WAFFLES

*This recipe also makes good pancakes, but it is not necessary to beat the egg whites separately. You can substitute different vegetables if desired. Serve with **Tasty Toppings**, page 125.*

2 eggs, separated
1 tbs. canola oil
1½ tsp. salt
1 tbs. honey, if desired

1 cup 2% milk
1 cup whole wheat flour
½ cup shredded carrots
1 cup finely chopped celery

Heat a waffle iron. Mix egg yolks with oil, salt, honey, if using, and milk. Add flour and beat well to blend. Stir in vegetables. Beat egg whites until stiff and fold into batter. Ladle onto waffle iron and close cover. Cook until waffle iron stops steaming and opens easily. Makes 6 to 8 waffles.

*per waffle* *151 calories, 6.4 g protein, 21.2 g carbo., 5.1 g fat, 29% calories from fat*

# FUNNY FACE PANCAKES

*This recipe shows how just a little extra effort can make the kids feel special. Cook the pancakes on a nonstick griddle or skillet, or use nonstick cooking spray to prepare the griddle. If desired, use ¾ cup egg substitute instead of eggs. Pick a **Tasty Topping** on page 125.*

3 eggs
1 cup low fat cottage cheese
¼ cup flour
dash salt, if desired

Beat eggs well. Add cottage cheese and beat. Add flour and salt, if using, and mix well. Fill a poultry baster with batter. Make a face with batter on a hot griddle: first the eyes, then nose and mouth. Cook for a few seconds. Ladle more batter over facial features and cook. Turn when brown on the first side. Continue to cook until done. Makes 4 to 6 pancakes.

---

***per pancake***   *90 calories, 8.9 g protein, 5.7 g carbo., 3.3 g fat, 34% calories from fat*

# PICKY-EATER PANCAKES

*Pour the batter onto a hot pan or griddle in a free form manner. After serving, ask your child to guess what you made. Whatever he or she guesses, of course, is right! Serve with **Tasty Toppings** on page 125.*

**TRY THIS**
1 small zucchini, sliced
1½ cups flour
3 tsp. baking powder
½ tsp. salt, if desired
1 egg, beaten
1 cup 2% milk
2 tbs. canola oil

**OR THIS**
1 small zucchini, sliced
1 cup pancake mix
¼ cup 2% milk
1 egg

Steam zucchini and puree in blender. Mix with remaining ingredients. Stir just until mixed. Cook pancakes on a hot pan or griddle, turning only once. Makes 8 to 10 pancakes.

*per pancake* 115 calories, 3.6 g protein, 16.3 g carbo., 3.9 g fat, 31% calories from fat

# TASTY TOPPINGS

*Get out of the butter-and-maple-syrup rut with one of these healthy toppings.*

- hot applesauce
- frozen berries, thawed and pureed with juice
- yogurt cheese or nonfat cream cheese, mixed with honey to taste
- flavored yogurt
- jam or preserves
- warm honey
- melted peanut butter (thin with apple juice, if desired)
- fresh fruit puree
- low fat cottage cheese
- shredded part-skim mozzarella cheese
- low fat or nonfat cream cheese and fresh fruit
- spiced pineapple: 1/4 cup crushed pineapple blended with 1 tsp. vanilla extract and 1/4 tsp. cinnamon

# FRUIT-N-CEREAL SQUARES

*These make a good breakfast on the run. They have a lot of calories to keep kids going throughout the morning.*

3 cups whole wheat flour
2 tsp. baking powder
¼ tsp. salt
3 cups quick oats

¼ cup honey
1½ cups margarine
2 cups jam or fruit puree

Combine flour, baking powder, salt, oats and honey. Cut in margarine until crumbly. Spread ⅔ of mixture on the bottom of an ungreased jelly roll pan (10-x-18-inches). Carefully spread mixture with jam. Sprinkle remaining ingredients over top. Bake at 350° for 30 minutes until lightly browned. Makes 12 servings.

*per serving*   *499 calories, 7.9 g protein, 78.7 g carbo., 19.1 g fat, 33% calories from fat*

# BREAKFAST BARS

*You can substitute rolled oats for the cereal in this high-protein, high-fiber morning square.*

1½ cups all-bran or granola cereal
¾ cup flour
1 tsp. baking powder
¼ tsp. salt, optional
¼ cup honey, or to taste

1 banana, mashed
½ cup margarine, melted
1 egg
1 tsp. vanilla extract

Set aside ½ cup of the cereal. Combine remaining ingredients in a bowl. Spread mixture into a greased 11-x-7-inch baking dish. Crush reserved cereal and sprinkle over batter. Bake at 350° for 25 minutes. Cool for a few minutes and cut into squares. Makes 12 servings.

*per serving* *177 calories, 4.1 g protein, 27.4 g carbo., 8.5 g fat, 38% calories from fat*

# EASY CINNAMON ROLLS

*Here's a sugarless way to make cinnamon rolls. Nonfat cream cheese mixed with apple butter makes a good frosting.*

1 loaf (11 oz.) frozen bread
   dough, thawed
¼ cup margarine
2 tbs. cinnamon

1 apple, chopped
1 cup raisins
½ cup pecans, optional

Roll dough into a 9-x-12-inch rectangle. Spread with margarine and sprinkle with cinnamon. Spread chopped apple, raisins and pecans, if desired, over dough. Roll up jelly roll-style. Cut into 1-inch slices. Place slices on a greased cookie sheet and let rise until they have nearly doubled in size. Bake at 350° for 25 to 35 minutes or until brown. Makes 12 servings.

*per roll*   146 calories, 3 g protein, 24.4 g carbo., 4.8 g fat, 30% calories from fat

# BREAKFAST BANANA SPLIT

*Make sure kids start the day right by disguising their morning cereal as dessert. Use fresh fruit that's in season, and always top it off with a cherry!*

½ cup low fat cottage cheese
1 tbs. honey
¼ cup strawberries or raspberries

½ cup low fat granola
1 banana, halved lengthwise
¼ cup mixed chopped fresh fruit

Mix cottage cheese and honey. Puree berries with a food processor or blender to resemble sauce. Reserve 1 tbs. of the granola. Put remaining granola in 2 banana-split dishes or bowls. Place 1 banana slice over each dish of granola. Scoop cottage cheese mixture with an ice cream scoop into the center of each banana slice. Drizzle berry "sauce" over cottage cheese and bananas. Scatter fresh fruit in dishes. Sprinkle top of cottage cheese with reserved granola to resemble nuts. Makes 2 servings.

*per serving*   294 calories, 23.2 g protein, 91 g carbo., 18 g fat, 27% calories from fat

# MARVELOUS MEALS

# SERVE A "POWER" LUNCH

Whether you have a preschooler who still has lunch at home or an older child who takes lunch to school, adding variety, excitement and a little color to lunch foods will get results you won't believe. Even if your little one doesn't go to school, occasionally pack lunch in a lunch box and see how it increases his or her interest in eating.

If you plan ahead, it takes only minutes to prepare something delicious and nutritious. Every meal can be something your child looks forward to. Try different combinations from various recipes in this chapter for more variety. Select a snack from *Super Snacks* to add to the lunch box fixings and complete the meal with one of the *Dynamite Drinks* for the vacuum bottle.

Help your child become more interested in trying new dishes by serving them with a flair. (No one has to know that tucked into an old favorite is a food usually left untouched.) If spaghetti is a favorite, sneak a little tuna or zucchini into the sauce. Introduce it by talking about Italy and the little boys and girls who live there. This gives the new dish a special image and your child not only learns about new foods, but also about new places and people. Who could resist trying something with all that going for it?

# MAMA MIA CUBES

*These are best when served cold. Secure cubes with frilly tooth-picks. Remove picks if serving them to small children, or replace them with pretzel sticks just before serving.*

8 thin slices extra-lean ham
1 medium cantaloupe

Cut ham into 1-inch strips. Cut cantaloupe into cubes. Wrap a ham strip around each cantaloupe cube and secure with toothpicks. Chill and serve. Makes 4 servings.

***per serving***   *121 calories, 12.2 g.protein, 11.7 g carbo., 3.2 g fat, 23% calories from fat*

# TOMATO BALLOONS

*These make a nice alternative to sandwiches. Kids will feel like grown-ups while they are eating them.*

1 medium tomato
¼ cup low fat cottage cheese
¼ cup water-packed tuna, drained

Cut stem end off tomato and scoop out insides. Mix cottage cheese and tuna. Stuff into tomato. Makes 1 serving.

*per serving*   *132 calories, 21.4 g protein, 7.7 g carbo., 1.7 g fat, 12% calories from fat*

# ADD PIZZAZZ TO PEANUT BUTTER

*Although peanut butter is delicious and nutritious, it gets about 70% of its calories from fat. Most national brands have a reduced fat version on the market which brings the fat content down to about 55%. If your child's plain peanut butter sandwich needs some liveliness, try adding one or more of the following.*

- chopped apple
- applesauce
- grated carrots
- chopped celery
- grated low fat or nonfat cheese
- minced cooked chicken breast
- unsweetened shredded coconut
- low fat cottage cheese
- yogurt cheese or nonfat cream cheese
- chopped dates

- extra-lean ham
- chopped dried fruit
- sliced pears
- crushed pineapple
- raisins
- crushed raspberries
- sesame seeds
- sprouts
- sunflower kernels
- diced tomatoes

# NUTCRACKER

*This mixture can also be served with carrot sticks and pear slices for dipping.*

1/2 cup yogurt cheese or nonfat cream cheese
1/4 cup crushed pineapple, well drained
1/4 cup chopped pecans
whole wheat crackers

Mix cheese, pineapple and pecans. Spread on wheat crackers. Makes 1 cup.

*per 1/4 cup filling*  *55.5 calories, 2.8 g protein, 6.3 g carbo., 2.4 g fat, 37% calories from fat*

# PINWHEELS

*Make these ahead of time and use as needed.*

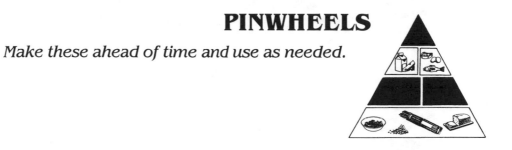

½ cup yogurt cheese or nonfat cream cheese, softened
1 tsp. Worcestershire sauce
½ tsp. chopped chives
¼ tsp. dry mustard
6 thin slices extra-lean ham
3 slices rye bread

Blend cheese, Worcestershire sauce, chives and mustard. Spread over ham slices and roll up jelly roll-style. Chill and cut into slices. Serve with rye bread. Makes 2 to 3 servings.

*per serving*  *146 calories, 14.4 g protein, 15 g carbo., 3.1 g fat, 19% calories from fat*

# APPLE PIE SANDWICH

*It contains fruit and vegetables, it's high in protein — yet it still tastes like dessert!*

¼ cup yogurt cheese or nonfat cream cheese
2 tbs. chopped walnuts
2 tbs. chopped celery
3 tbs. chopped apple
1 tsp. cinnamon
4 slices raisin bread

Mix cheese, walnuts, celery, apple and cinnamon. Spread on 2 slices of the raisin bread. Top with remaining bread slices. Makes 2 servings.

***per serving*** *197 calories, 7.2 g protein, 34.5 g carbo., 3.9 g fat, 17% calories from fat*

# THANKSGIVING SANDWICH

*This sandwich lets you celebrate turkey day any time.*

½ cup chopped cooked turkey
2-3 tbs. yogurt cheese or nonfat cream cheese
2 tbs. cranberry sauce
4 slices whole wheat bread

Mix turkey with cheese and cranberry sauce. Spread on 2 slices of the bread. Top with remaining bread slices. Makes 2 servings.

*per serving*   *334 calories, 19.3 g protein, 40.7 g carbo., 11.7 g fat, 30% calories from fat*

# PIRANHA PITA POCKET

*Sardines are a good source of calcium. Substitute water-packed tuna, if desired.*

4 sardines, chopped
2 tbs. sweet pickle relish
2 tbs. reduced fat mayonnaise
¼ cup grated Monterey Jack cheese
2 small pita breads

Mix sardines, relish, mayonnaise and cheese. Cut a 1-inch section from one side of each pita bread to open a pocket. Place cut section of bread inside pocket. Spoon sardine mixture into pita pockets. Makes 2 servings.

***per serving*** *309 calories, 15.8 g protein, 39 g carbo., 9.9 g fat, 29% calories from fat*

# FANCY HAM SANDWICH

*The combination of bright colors and fancy designs in this sandwich will entice the kids to eat it all.*

2 drops food coloring
1 tbs. 2% milk
4 slices oatmeal bread
¼ cup cooked peas, mashed
3 oz. extra-lean ham, finely chopped
2 tbs. reduced fat mayonnaise

Mix food coloring with milk and lightly paint a design on 2 slices of the bread. Toast all bread slices lightly. Mix peas with ham and mayonnaise. Spread mixture on the plain toast slices and top with decorated slices, design-side up. Makes 2 servings.

---

***per serving***   *267 calories, 17.1 g protein, 38 g carbo., 6.3 g fat, 20% calories from fat*

# HAM AND CHEESE PILLOWS

*Substitute chopped cooked chicken breast for ham and add a little celery for crunch.*

3 oz. extra-lean ham, finely chopped
1 tbs. reduced fat mayonnaise
¼ cup grated Monterey Jack cheese
2 small pita breads

Mix ham, mayonnaise and cheese. Cut a 1-inch section from one side of each pita bread to open a pocket. Place cut sections of bread inside pockets. Spoon ham mixture into pita pockets. Makes 2 servings.

*per serving*  294 calories, 18.1 g protein, 34.2 g carbo., 9.2 g fat, 28% calories from fat

# VEGGIE PILLOWS

*Use a combination of chopped celery, carrots, green peppers and mushrooms for a crunchy, colorful lunch.*

¼ cup bean sprouts
¼ cup chopped vegetables
1 tbs. ranch-style salad dressing
1 small pita bread

Combine bean sprouts, chopped vegetables and dressing in a bowl. Cut a 1-inch section from one side of pita bread to open a pocket. Place cut sections of bread inside pockets. Stuff veggie mixture into pita pocket. Makes 1 to 2 servings.

*per serving*   *227 calories, 7.2 g protein, 35.2 g carbo., 6.6 g fat, 26% calories from fat*

# MOZZARELLA MUFFINS

*French or rye bread rounds make good substitutes for English muffins.*

¼ cup grated part-skim mozzarella cheese
2 tbs. reduced fat mayonnaise
2 English muffins, halved

Mix cheese with mayonnaise and spread on muffin halves. Broil until cheese is bubbly. Makes 2 servings.

*per serving*   *196 calories, 8.1 g protein, 27.3 g carbo., 5.3 g fat, 25% calories from fat*

# NEW ENGLAND MUFFINS

*Stick two of these together and tuck them into the lunch box.*

¼ cup grated cheddar cheese
¼ cup grated apple
2 English muffins, halved

Mix together cheese and apples. Sprinkle evenly on muffin halves. Broil until bubbly or bake at 350° for 10 minutes. Makes 2 servings.

*per serving   205 calories, 8.1 g protein, 28.5 g carbo., 5.8 g fat, 26% calories from fat*

# NACHO SANDWICH

*Instead of sour cream, garnish this with yogurt cheese diluted with a little nonfat (skim) milk. Look for low fat or nonfat refried beans. They're often labeled vegetarian.*

2 flour tortillas, warmed
½ cup vegetarian refried beans, heated
¼ cup grated cheddar cheese
¼ cup shredded lettuce
¼ cup chopped tomato

Spread tortillas evenly with beans. Top equally with remaining ingredients. Fold over one end of each tortilla and roll up sideways. Makes 2 servings.

*per serving*   224 calories, 10.2 g protein, 31 g carbo., 7.7 g fat, 30% calories from fat

# TUNA BOATS

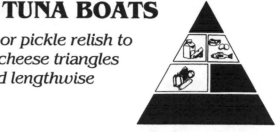

*Add seeds, grated carrots, chopped celery or pickle relish to tuna mixture for an added attraction. Cheddar cheese triangles make neat sails. Or use fat carrots thinly sliced lengthwise and cut into triangles.*

1 can (6½ oz.) water-packed tuna, drained
1½ tbs. plain low fat yogurt
1 small green bell pepper

Mix tuna with yogurt and any other desired ingredients. Cut green pepper in half (or in quarters for a small child), lengthwise. Remove seeds and membranes. Fill with tuna mixture. Add sails, if desired. Makes 2 servings.

***per serving*** *137 calories, 25.8 g protein, 6.3 g carbo., 0.6 g fat, 4% calories from fat*

# PIZZA GOBBLER

*Use your child's favorite vegetable as an additional topping.*

½ cup pizza sauce
4 English muffins, halved
¼ cup grated part-skim mozzarella cheese
1 turkey frankfurter, sliced

   Spread sauce evenly on muffin halves. Sprinkle each half with cheese and top with frankfurter slices. Broil until cheese is bubbly. Makes 4 servings.

*per serving*   *217 calories, 8.4 g protein, 31.5 g carbo., 5.7 g fat, 24% calories from fat*

# BAHAMA BAGELS

*Offer your brown-bagger this nice change of pace.*

½ cup low fat cottage cheese
1 tsp. chopped walnuts
1 tsp. crushed pineapple
2 bagels, halved

Mix cheese, pineapple and nuts. Spread between bagel slices. Makes 2 servings.

*per serving* *245 calories, 15.1 g protein, 37.7 g carbo., 3.3 g fat, 12% calories from fat*

# ADD TEMPTATION TO TUNA

*Tired tuna can be made tasty and tempting with a few of these additions.*

- sliced almonds
- chopped apples
- cooked and crumbled turkey bacon
- green beans
- bean sprouts
- chopped celery
- shredded cabbage
- grated low fat or nonfat cheese
- chow mein noodles
- cooked pasta
- grapes
- diced bell peppers
- Mandarin orange segments
- peas
- pickle slices
- crushed pineapple
- diced tomatoes
- yogurt cheese or nonfat cream cheese
- chopped walnuts
- sliced water chestnuts

# TUNA PILLOWS

*Cornbread, onions and olives enliven traditional tuna casserole.*

1 pkg. (10 oz.) cornbread mix
1 tbs. dehydrated minced onion
1 can (6½ oz.) water-packed tuna, drained
¼ cup chopped black olives

Prepare cornbread batter according to package directions. Stir in tuna and onion. Pour into a greased 10-x-15-inch jelly roll pan. Scatter olives over top. Bake at 400° for 15 to 20 minutes. Cut into squares. Makes 12 servings.

***per serving*** *103 calories, 6.3 g protein, 12.4 g carbo., 3.1 g fat, 27% calories from fat*

# POPOVERS

*Here's a way to present a lunch that fascinates children. Popovers lend themselves to any kind of spread and they tempt a child to try something different. Liquid egg substitute reduces fat and cholesterol and keeps well in the refrigerator or freezer. Serve popovers hot with your favorite spread. Split them open to stuff with a filling.*

1 cup flour
1/2 tsp. salt
1 cup 2% milk
1/2 cup egg substitute, or 2 eggs

Spray muffin cups well with nonstick cooking spray. Place in a 425° oven to heat. Beat ingredients together just until smooth. Fill heated muffin cups 3/4 full. Bake for 40 to 45 minutes or until golden brown. Do not open oven during baking. Serve immediately or fill with a savory filling. Makes 6 popovers.

***per popover*** *102 calories, 5.1 g protein, 17 g carbo., 1 g fat, 11% calories from fat*

# TUNARONI STUFFERS

*This high protein, high carbohydrate meal provides lots of energy for active kids. Make them laugh by using funny pasta shapes instead of macaroni.*

1 can (6½ oz.) water-packed tuna, drained
1 cup cooked macaroni
2½ tbs. plain low fat yogurt
½ tbs. mustard
4 *Popovers*, page 152

Combine tuna, macaroni, yogurt and mustard. Spoon into popovers. Serve immediately. Makes 4 servings.

---

***per serving***   *206 calories, 18.2 g protein, 22.7 g carbo., 4.1 g fat, 18% calories from fat*

# KINGFISH STUFFERS

*Any filling tastes twice as good served in a popover shell.*

1 can (6½ oz.) water-packed tuna, drained
2 tbs. plain low fat yogurt
1 tbs. chopped apple
1 tbs. grated carrots
1 tbs. raisins
4 *Popovers*, page 152

Combine tuna, yogurt, apple, carrot and raisins. Fill popovers with mixture. Serve immediately. Makes 4 servings.

*per serving*  *162 calories, 16.4 g protein, 14.8 g carbo., 3.8 g fat, 22% calories from fat*

# SCRAPPLE STUFFERS

*Apple butter contains no butter at all. It is made by slowly cooking together apples, spices and cider.*

¼ cup apple butter
¼ cup grated cheddar cheese
4 *Popovers*, page 152

Heat apple butter gently in a small saucepan. Divide apple butter equally among warm popovers. Top with cheese. Serve immediately. Makes 4 servings.

***per serving*** *77 calories, 2.4 g protein, 10.3 g carbo., 3.1 g fat, 35% calories from fat*

# CHINESE CHICKEN STUFFERS

*Feeding your kids exotic flavors when they are young will make them adventurous eaters as adults.*

½ cup chopped cooked chicken
2-3 tbs. drained crushed pineapple
¼ cup chopped snow peas
2 tbs. plain nonfat yogurt
¼ cup chow mein noodles
4 *Popovers*, page 152

Combine chicken, pineapple, snow peas and yogurt in a small saucepan. Heat on low until just warmed through. Remove from heat and stir in noodles. Fill warm popovers and serve immediately. Makes 4 servings.

---

***per serving*** *159 calories, 9.7 g protein, 16.7 g carbo., 5.8 g fat, 33% calories from fat*

# TURKEY CIRCLES

*Hot dogs in hamburger buns? This special cooking technique will leave your kids wondering, "How did she do that?"*

4 turkey frankfurters
4 hamburger buns
1 can (8 oz.) baked beans

   Slash each frankfurter crosswise at ½-inch intervals, cutting halfway through. Broil or barbecue frankfurter until it curls into a circle and is heated through. Toast buns. Place a frankfurter circle on the bottom half of each bun. Fill centers of circles with 2 tbs. baked beans. Cover with top bun. Serve remaining beans as a side dish. Makes 4 servings.

*per serving*   285 calories, 13.1 g protein, 34.2 g carbo., 10.9 g fat, 34% calories from fat

# POPEYE BURGERS

*Use any vegetable to enrich burgers. It's sneaky, but it works!*

1 cup spinach
1 lb. ground turkey
6 hamburger buns

Steam spinach and puree with a blender. Add to ground turkey and mix lightly but well. Form into patties and broil. Serve on toasted buns. Makes 6 servings.

*per serving*  304 calories, 22.4 g protein, 22.8 g carbo., 12.8 g fat, 39% calories from fat

# CORNY PUDDING

*Here's an unusual way to serve a popular vegetable. Most major brands offer canned vegetables without added salt. If you buy regular canned vegetables, rinse them first to remove excess salt.*

2 eggs
1 cup water
1 can (16 oz.) whole kernel corn
1 cup dates, finely chopped

Lightly beat eggs in a bowl. Add water and stir to blend. Place corn and dates in a saucepan. Stir in egg mixture. Cook over low heat for 15 minutes. Pour into a blender container. Blend on high speed until smooth. Return to saucepan and cook for 10 minutes, stirring constantly. Pour into individual serving dishes and chill in refrigerator. Makes 4 servings.

*per serving*  *251 calories, 7 g protein, 53.8 g carbo., 3.8 g fat, 12% calories from fat*

# POPEYE'S PIE

*This was the one that made a spinach lover out of Popeye.*

1 pkg. (10 oz.) refrigerator pizza dough
1 lb. fresh spinach, steamed, or frozen spinach, thawed
1 egg
⅓ cup wheat germ
¼ cup grated Swiss or cheddar cheese
1 tsp. Worcestershire sauce
pinch garlic powder

Heat oven to 400°. Unroll pizza dough. Reshape dough to line a 9-inch pie pan. Combine spinach, egg, wheat germ, cheese, Worcestershire sauce and garlic powder. Pour into pizza shell. Bake for 25 minutes. Cut into wedges. Makes 6 servings.

*per serving*   *188 calories, 9.7 g protein, 27.7 g carbo., 4.9 g fat, 23% calories from fat*

# MEXICAN WIENERS

*This one is fun for kids to make and eat. Serve with mild salsa.*

1 turkey frankfurter
2 tbs. vegetarian refried beans
¼ cup shredded lettuce
1 tbs. grated cheddar cheese
1 flour or corn tortilla

Cook turkey frankfurter according to package directions. Spread refried beans on tortilla. Sprinkle with lettuce and cheese. Place frankfurter close to one side. Roll tortilla around frankfurter. Warm in a microwave or oven and serve. Or serve at room temperature. Makes 1 serving.

*per serving*   *266 calories, 12.7 g protein, 25.9 g carbo., 13.1 g fat, 43% calories from fat*

# SKINNY DIPS

*My son could eat these every night! Now he helps me prepare them.*

4 large potatoes, baked
½ cup grated part-skim mozzarella cheese
2 oz. extra-lean ham, diced
1 green onion, chopped
½ cup ranch-style salad dressing

Cut potatoes in half lengthwise. Scoop out most of potato and reserve for another recipe. Sprinkle cheese, ham and green onion over skins. Heat in a 350° oven for 4 to 5 minutes, until cheese is bubbly. Serve with dressing for dipping. Makes 4 servings.

*per serving*   *396 calories, 12.6 g protein, 55.6 g carbo., 14.5 g fat, 32% calories from fat*

## VARIATIONS
## MEXICAN SKINNY DIPS

Sprinkle potato skins with ½ cup grated part-skim mozzarella cheese, 2 slices cooked and crumbled turkey sausage and 1 chopped green onion. Dip in salsa.

*per serving*   *308 calories, 11.4 g protein, 55.6 g carbo., 5.2 g fat, 15% calories from fat*

## PIZZA SKINNY DIPS

Sprinkle potato skins with ¼ cup grated part-skim mozzarella cheese, ¼ cup grated Parmesan cheese, 2 oz. diced turkey salami and 1 chopped green onion. Dip in pizza sauce.

*per serving*   *306 calories, 11.7 g protein, 56.4 g carbo., 5.6 g fat, 13% calories from fat*

# EAT YOUR SPINACH

*Substitute broccoli for spinach or try another vegetable. Prepare the casserole with nonstick cooking spray to keep the fat content low. Add a little 2% milk to the spinach mixture if it appears too thick.*

1 pkg. (10 oz.) frozen chopped spinach
1 pkg. (3 oz.) nonfat cream cheese, softened
½ cup breadcrumbs
¼ cup grated Parmesan cheese
1 tsp. salt, or to taste

Cook spinach according to package directions. Drain well. Mix spinach, cream cheese and salt. Place in a greased casserole. Toss breadcrumbs and cheese in a bowl. Sprinkle over spinach mixture. Bake at 350° for 30 minutes. Makes 4 servings.

---

***per serving*** *121 calories, 8.8 g protein, 16.4 g carbo., 2.7 g fat, 19% calories from fat*

---

# SPAGHETTI SALAD

*Here's an Italian way of serving vegetables. Top with grated Parmesan cheese if desired. Use whole wheat or vegetable spaghetti for variety. Use any combination of sliced cooked carrots, zucchini, green beans, green pepper or other favorites for the vegetables.*

½ cups plain nonfat yogurt
1 tbs. lemon juice
1 tsp. Italian seasoning herbs
½ lb. spaghetti, cooked and well-drained
½ cup chopped celery
2 tbs. chopped green onion, if desired
2 cups sliced cooked vegetables

Mix yogurt, lemon juice and herbs together well. Combine spaghetti, celery, green onion, if using, and vegetables in a large mixing bowl. Toss with yogurt mixture. Chill before serving. Makes 4 to 6 servings.

---

*per serving*   185 calories, 10.4 g protein, 35.5 g carbo., 0.7 g fat, 3% calories from fat

# PETITE APPLE TARTS

*Complaints from the family that there's never any dessert? Try these easy, low fat treats.*

2 tbs. cornstarch
1 tsp. cinnamon
¼ tsp. nutmeg
1 cup frozen apple juice concentrate

1 tbs. lemon juice
1 tbs. margarine
6 cups sliced unpeeled apples
6 individual graham cracker crusts

Blend cornstarch, cinnamon, nutmeg, apple juice concentrate and lemon juice together in a saucepan. Cook over medium heat until thickened. Add margarine. Divide apple slices evenly in crusts. Pour slightly cooled apple juice mixture over apples. Bake in a 350° oven for 30 to 40 minutes. Makes 6 servings.

*per serving*   *477 calories, 3 g protein, 81.5 g carbo., 17.1 g fat, 31% calories from fat*

# INDEX

# Serve creative, easy, nutritious meals with nitty gritty® cookbooks

9x13 Pan Cookbook, The
100 Dynamite Desserts
Beer and Good food
Best Bagels are Made at Home, The
Best Pizza is Made at Home, The
Bread Baking
Bread Machine Cookbook II, The
Bread Machine Cookbook III, The
Bread Machine Cookbook IV, The
   Whole Grains & Natural Sugars
Bread Machine Cookbook V, The
Favorite Recipes from 100 Kitchens
Bread Machine Cookbook VI, The
Hand-Shaped Breads from the
Dough Cycle
Bread Machine Cookbook, The
Cappuccino/Espresso:
   The Book of Beverages
Casseroles
Coffee Book, The
Convection Oven Cookery
Cooking for 1 or 2
Cooking in Clay
Cooking with Chile Peppers
Cooking with Fresh Herbs

Cooking with Grains
Creative Mexican Cooking
Deep Fried Indulgences
Dehydrator Cookbook, The
Easy Vegetarian Cooking
Edible Pockets for Every Meal
Entrées from Your Bread Machine
Extra-Special Crockery Pot Recipes
Favorite Cookie Recipes
Favorite Seafood Recipes
Fresh Vegetables
From Freezer, 'Fridge and Pantry
From Your Ice Cream Maker
Garlic Cookbook, The
Gourmet Gifts
Healthy Cooking on the Run
Healthy Snack for Kids
Juicer Book I and II, The
Low Fat American Favorites
Marinades
Muffins, Nut Breads and More
New Blender Book, The
New International Fondue Cookbook
No Salt, No Sugar, No Fat Cookbook
One Dish Meals

Oven and Rotisserie Roasting
Party Fare:
   Irresistible Nibbles for
   Every Occasion
Pasta Machine Cookbook, The
Quick and Easy Pasta Recipes
Recipes for the Loaf Pan
Recipes for the Pressure Cooker
Recipes for Yogurt Cheese
Risottos, Paellas and Other Rice
   Specialties
Sandwich Maker Cookbook, The
Sautés
Skewer Cooking on the Grill
Slow Cooking
Steamer Cookbook, The
Toaster Oven Cookbook, The
Unbeatable Chicken Recipes
Versatile Rice Cooker, The
Waffles
Well Dressed Potato, The
Wok, The
Worldwide Sourdoughs from Your
   Bread Machine
Wraps and Roll-ups

For a free catalog, write or call: **Bristol Publishing Enterprises, Inc.**
P.O. Box 1737, San Leandro, CA 94577  (800)346-4889